T0067114

Raising Godly Children

Itakpe Theophilus

authorHOUSE®

AuthorHouse™
1663 Liberty Drive
Bloomington, IN 47403
www.authorhouse.com
Phone: 1 (800) 839-8640

Published by AuthorHouse   02/05/2015

ISBN: 978-1-4969-6804-3 (sc)
ISBN: 978-1-4969-6803-6 (e)

Library of Congress Control Number: 2015901702

"Train up a child in the way he should go, and when he is old, he will not depart from it."

– Proverbs 22:6 (KJV)

Dedication

This book is dedicated to lovers and seekers of truth everywhere who are passionately disposed to the uplifting of God's kingdom work in our much-wicked world of today.

It is also dedicated to my friend, Mr. Chris Ohwo, for his immense support in my time of distress, and particularly for helping me regain confidence after a traumatic experience.

Contents

Acknowledgements

Wherever it was found necessary in the course of writing this book, in order that a point raised was well-buttressed, I made reference to an opinion or an idea that had been expressed in a published book. The following books are hereby acknowledged:

1. *Commentary on the Whole Bible*, Matthew Henry, *(Hendrickson)*
2. *The Power of Thinking Big*, John C. Maxwell, *(River Oak)*
3. *The Pursuit of God*, A. W. Tozer, *(Christian Pub. Cam Hill)*
4. *Jesus the Healer*, E. W. Kenyon, *(Kenyon Gospel Publishing Society)*
5. *Jesus the Healer*, E. W. Kenyon, *(Kenyon Gospel Publishing Society)*

Introduction

Raising a godly child, nay, bringing him up in the best way possible, according to God's prescribed standards for human beings, is one God-given task that people have not fully learnt how best to handle with confidence. As a result of this, the issue has never stopped stirring much anxiety in the minds of many people in every generation since time immemorial. The craving today, even as ever before, by every parent is to be able to have every child received from God raised in the best way possible – as a disciplined, godly and obedient child capable of attaining success ultimately. Because, by so doing, it is hoped our society would be made much better to the delight of our creator.

Following this, Christians, and indeed human beings in general, have kept wondering about how best to excel with raising a child. That is, to raise a child the best way possible, or at least, score high marks as per our God's standards set out for us. I tell you, friend, that it absolutely possible to have every child born into the world raised as a godly child. Realize that, as a matter of fact, our God does not expect anything less from us. What I have set out to do on the pages of this book therefore is to show how to have a perfect blend of both the spiritual exercises that our growing children should be made to undergo, and the training in moral rectitude that they need in order to grow up to become godly children. Know that these spiritual exercises and moral lessons must be on the bedrock of Jesus the savior. Recall that He (Jesus) had said in the Scriptures that no human being can ever succeed in any endeavor without Him – John 15:6.

According to Matthew Henry, in his commentary on the whole Bible, "Jesus is the beginning, the middle, and the end of every one's life". He said, "In Jesus every human being born into the world must set out, go on, and finish" He emphasized that, because Jesus is the only truth there is in this whole world, He alone is the sure guide of our every way, and because He is the embodiment of life, He is undoubtedly the unquestionable end of everyone's life. I was really thrilled by this very intelligent submission of Matthew Henry's.

And so, in line with what he said; I agree that people must understand that before childbearing commences, there is need to contract formal unions, and to endeavor to live righteously. Because, this would always present the right platform for every child born into the family to grow the godly way.

With a decent Christian background, the issue of making Jesus the beginning, the middle, and the end of our children's lives would not always be a difficult task to achieve.

My work in this book therefore is designed to point the right way to have our children fed with the only true bread in the world; wherein lies the genuine truth. Understand that any child fed with this bread of life stands insured for ultimate success at the end of his godly walk, see John 6: 35.

I assure you that you will be better equipped with the ''how- to'' make Jesus the beginning, the middle, and the end of your child's life after you have read this book.

Chapter One

Be Godly To Raise Godly Children

Children are usually molded by the words they hear and in some cases, the ones they should have heard, and didn't. When a child is raised in a family where godly virtues such as care, love, humility, etc., are esteemed, the child will grow up a better person than one raised in a secular household.

And it's certainly not disputable that when a child's parents begin to inculcate moral and Christian values in their offspring from a young age, the child will more likely live righteously, and in the fear of God, when he or she is an adult.

Children, generally, are very good at copying and imitating what they see. The child will copy the parents' lifestyle, no doubt. Parents must therefore endeavor to always live exemplary lives. By this I am insinuating that your child will be decent and godly if you as a parent are decent and godly. Because, essentially, what the child becomes ultimately in life is a function of the quality of the training he or she got from the home.

I tell you friend that whatever lessons your child learned, or didn't learn but should have, while growing up determine what he or she becomes. And the child who was taught the good lessons about God and righteous living will always love his or her parents for it.

Hear the confession made by Bob Gass, an Irish-born-American preacher, and author of many books, including Starting Over which confirms this assertion:

"The things I learned from watching her affected me more than all the books I've ever read, and all the sermons I've ever listened to. Some of the kids I grew up with on the streets of Belfast joined sectarian organizations, and ended up in prison or dead. But she took God in one hand and us {Bob and his siblings} in the other, and announced; "As for me and my house, we will serve the Lord."

Bob Gass revealed in his book that what they, he and his siblings, learned from their mother as she raised them alone following their father's death, Gass was twelve at the time, had paid off. He stated with excitement that he and his elder brother ended up working in the Ministry, while his younger sister became a Christian writer.

At this point, let me attempt to discuss some critical issues that people, parents and would-be parents alike, should examine deeply before child-bearing begins. I understand clearly that these are usually the major issues that would often affect how a child is raised in a home:

1. Are You Spiritually Mature For Childbearing?

Many people, I discovered, do not understand that there is the need for someone to be spiritually mature in order to be able to perceive things of God. They simply do not realize that God programs all aspects of their lives according to His divine arrangement. The Lord said in the scriptures; "The right time for me has not yet come; for you anytime is right" (John 7:6, 2:4).

The obvious lesson the Lord had rightly taught with this statement is that, it is extremely important for us to mature spiritually. You certainly would fair better if you have the capacity and necessary ability to discern things of God properly before going into certain spiritual undertakings in life, such as marriage. You will not be able to discern your God-given dreams, for instance, if you are not born again and are spiritually mature.

Observe that Abraham and Sarah, his wife, had only reacted the way they did, as recorded in Genesis 17:17 and 18:12, according to their understanding of the spiritual matters of God. We read in these Scriptures' respective accounts that they laughed heartily at God's promise of a son to them. But on the contrary, instead of laughing and trivializing God's similar promise of a son to her, Mary, the Lord's mother had displayed a commendable sense of spiritual understanding in matters of God when she had received similar good news from heaven. Hear how she had responded:

"I am the Lord's servant, May it be to me as you have said."
Luke 1:38.

Know that you will not succeed in your marriage unless you have enough spiritual insight to choose your right partner. And you will not be able to raise your child as a godly child unless you are mature enough spiritually. Try to understand the special or peculiar traits of the child God has given you like Mary is recorded to have done while raising the boy Jesus.

I believe Mary was able to work with God in raising her son Jesus as a godly child because, according to Luke 2:51b; "But his mother treasured all these things [what was said about him and every unusual things he did] in her heart". The Lord's mother never, for once, trivialized any display of unusual courage, wisdom and intelligence by the boy Jesus while He was growing up, as in Luke 2:47 – 49. Once, she had even had to prevail on her son, Jesus, to perform His first miracle of turning water into wine, John 2:1-11; thereby rightly demonstrating that she knew who He was; and that she understood that He had the miracle-working power of God in Him to do supernatural things.

2. Are You Also Old Enough?

"A person's age is only a number." I hear people say this all the time, or, "Age is nothing more than a mere number which is simply a thing of the mind." I have always believed this myself, until recently when I came to understand otherwise.

With men, one's age may just be a number and simply a thing of the mind; but not with God. Everything God made in His universe He programmed according to His timing; even the age of every human being. Observe in Ecclesiastes 3:2 where Solomon had revealed that it is God who sets the time for everyone to be born and to die. And the Psalmist had agreed that, indeed, it is God who ordains the date and day of everyone's birth, Psalm 139:16.

The Christian who is born again, mature spiritually, and advanced in age would find it more convenient living in conformity with God's rules. Know that there is a predetermined time for every activity in your life. Making major decisions pertaining to issues like when to marry, who to marry, how many children to be brought into the world, etc. you would do with better precision or accuracy when you walk with God. In other words, when you rely on God, your absolute fulfillment, happiness and victory in all your earthly endeavors is ensured.

Remember that the Lord had hesitated before exercising His miracle-working power to get water changed into wine at His mother's request, because, as He said; "my time has not yet come" John 2:4. Jesus knew the times, no doubt; but, because He didn't want to be seen as not dividing the times rightly, hence, He had reproved His mother here.

The other day, I listened to (Dr.) David Oyedepo, president and founder of Living Faith Church (A.K.A. Winners Chapel) here in Nigeria, in a sermon titled "Bible Sense for Marriage" where he said; "marriage isn't for boys and girls, but for young men and young ladies." He explained that if a young man preparing for marriage can't afford the cost of his wedding suit; and the young lady also, her wedding gown, then, they had better had a rethink, whether to wait for a more auspicious time or to go ahead and marry, nonetheless.

I agree with Dr. Oyedepo, because a marriage not well planned for would always produce offspring not equally planned for at the end of the day. It is only when a tree is good that it can bear good fruit, Matthews 7:17. The craze today in our societies is for people to impatiently rush into marriages, or for even unmarried people to indulge in indiscriminate sexual activities, without any proper plan made by anyone to have the products of the relationships bred as responsible and disciplined children. And when this happens, our societies become the worse for it—they become littered with "unwanted elements."

I looked into the Bible and found that, somehow, old-testament saints were never given to the kind of impatience exhibited by us today. For instance, Isaac, God's child of promise to Abraham, had married his wife, Rebecca at the ripe age of forty (see Genesis 25:20).

Esau married his own wife at the same age too, Genesis 26:34.

And we read also that Moses had married his midianite wife, Zipporah, when he was well over forty years old. Believers should, therefore, understand that maturity often makes for success in our Christian or godly work and walk.

You should know that God is in charge of your life, and time is your friend. Patience is the weapon that always forces deception to the surface. Perception is what you do need to discern God's timing for you. Give God a chance to work on your behalf according to His plan.

3. Are You Economically Stable?

It is not just enough to bring children into the world indiscriminately without planning beforehand for their future. Your delight in bearing a child must be matched with a corresponding passion to raise the child afterwards in the best way possible. And to be able to raise your child in the best way possible, all other things being equal, would require that you have a basic level of economic stability or a basic level of financial power.

Note that, over and above everything else, parental neglect occasioned, in most cases, by financial incapability is the root cause of so many of the social vices in our societies today. You find young boys taking to robbery, or young girls indulging in prostitution, for want of something more dignifying to do in order that they could fend for themselves where their parents are not able. This is an ugly trend that does not always augur well for our world community. Meanwhile, Paul had taught that it doesn't tell well of the Christian not to be able to fend for his family:

But if any provide not for his own, and specially for those of his own house, he hath denied the faith, and is worse than an infidel – 1 Timothy 5:8 (KJV).

I believe people will do better with children upbringing if they ever take pain to evaluate their strengths and weaknesses, financially and otherwise, before marriage and procreation. The irony today, however, is that people of "low-income", or "no-income" value at all, often take the lead when it comes to bringing children into the world.

Remember that Jacob and Moses had had to work for their fathers-in-law to be able to meet with the demands of taking in their wives – See Genesis 29 and Exodus 2. In other words, these men had ensured that they were gainfully employed and were, somewhat, stable financially, before they took their spouses.

And although nothing is recorded in the scriptures as to the end of the lives of Moses' children, it is, however, common knowledge that Jacob's offspring had gained enormous favor from God ultimately: He turned them, the children of one man, into His own chosen nation on earth.

4. Are You Morally/Emotionally Stable?

To be stable morally and emotionally is important for our godly walk. This is part of the reason the Lord Jesus had taught the world the famous one man, one wife rule in Matthew Chapter 19. And the Apostle Paul later did well to expound it vividly in the scriptures as quoted below – Observe that Paul's teaching here is on the implications of marrying just a wife, let alone, to marry many women:

But those who marry will face many troubles in this life, and I want to spare you this....

I would like you to be free from concern. An unmarried man is concerned about the Lord's affairs—how he can please the Lord.

But a married man is concerned about the affairs of this world – how he can please his wife and his interests are divided.

An unmarried woman or virgin is concerned about the Lord's affairs: Her aim is to be devoted to the Lord in both body and spirit.

But a married woman is concerned about the affairs of this world – how she can please her husband – 1 Corinthians 7:28a, 32 – 34.

Paul says marriage would not let the married individual live in the best way possible with his/her God; because it often leads to divided devotion, see verse 35. And, of a truth, we read in the scriptures that Solomon, because he was involved with a multitude of women, was the reason he had strayed from God's ideals during his reign as king over ancient Israel.

As a result of which, even though God had favored him with greater riches and wisdom than all the other kings of the earth during his time, 1 Kings 10:23, he allowed himself to be led far away from God by his numerous wives, most of whom were foreigners who worshipped other gods and had different standards of right and wrong. It was therefore not a surprise that, ultimately, because of his wives' religions, he had built shrines and encouraged pagan worship right in Jerusalem, God's holy city.

We should learn, from Solomon's story above, how unbridled appetite for sexual satisfaction could cause someone a derailment from his destiny pathway. It will usually cause an individual some moral or emotional instability to the extent that he/she is not able to master his/her affairs quite squarely; let alone be able to succeed.

5. Do You Have the Spiritual Insight/Initiative to Integrate Your Child Properly Into the Society?

Here, let me simply cite a story from the scriptures of a couple who had successfully worked with God in raising a godly child. It is the story of the birth of Samuel in first Samuel Chapter One. The Bible records that Samuel's mother, Hannah, had agonized for a very long while over her state of childlessness. And in desperation, Hannah had turned to God for help praying and promising to dedicate her son to Him.

So, in the cause of time, Hannah conceived and gave birth to a son, whom she named Samuel. And she didn't hesitate to fulfill the vow she had made to the Lord in 1 Samuel 1:11; as she had given up her little boy, after he was weaned, to live his whole life worshiping God in the home of an aged priest named Eli – 1 Samuel 1:28.

Observe that Hannah did not only show that she had a good understanding of the things of God here in this story; she, indeed, also showed that she possessed a high level of initiative to work with God in the upbringing of her son as a godly child. Because, in the end, it was this single event that made the remarkable difference between Samuel's life and the lives of Hophni and Phinehas, priest Eli's sons. Hannah, Samuel's mother, had had the understanding to integrate Samuel properly into the society, thus, paving the way for his rise from obscurity to prominence.

The world still celebrate Hannah for her action today, because, Samuel, as we have read in the Scriptures, eventually grew into one of the greatest leaders Israel ever knew; a fact which is no less true even till date. But Eli's sons had been destroyed because of their notoriety in waywardness.

As parents, it is our duty to be able to differentiate, in specific terms, our children's physical needs from those regarded as emotional needs; and to be able to separate both from their spiritual needs. And unless you do have the spiritual insight and initiative, like Samuel's parents above, to put your child where he/she would be adequately groomed in matters of God, like the boy Samuel was, it will simply be impossible to raise your child as a godly child.

The word of God is the tool with which you mold your child. Paul says; "All scripture is God-breathed, and is useful for teaching, rebuking, correcting, and training in righteousness; so that the man (child) of God maybe thoroughly equipped for every good work,"2 Timothy 3:16 – 17.

Chapter Two

A Formal Holy Union is Where To Start

"That everyone may eat and drink, and find satisfaction in all his toil" – this is the gift of God to every human being, Ecclesiastes 3:13. But when we look around our societies today and see how people indulge unscrupulously in indiscriminate and pervasive sexual activities; one is almost tempted to conclude that sex forms part of the gift of God to humanity as revealed in the scripture above to be indulged in at will by everyone.

People do not seem to realize that sex is a sacred act our God had sanctioned only for two persons in a marital relationship. Observe that at the beginning, first, God had created the man and the woman, Genesis 1:27, and afterwards He blessed them, and granted them divine authority to relate sexually only because they were in a formal union. This was so that the earth might be replenished as they procreate,

Genesis 1:28.

I call sex by two persons in a marital relationship "a sacred act" because God expects that, through it, a strong bond of oneness between a husband and his wife will always be provided. In other words, sex is expected to make the man and woman involved in matrimony always feel special to each other in accordance with God's word in Genesis 2:24; because it affords them that special avenue to express their love and warmth towards one another.

Now, why did God sanction sex as a sacred act between a man and a woman duly married? A lot of human beings never bother to find this truth before indulging in indiscriminate sex, and this is the reason the sexual sin is about the most rampant sin in our world today.

People must observe that there are three basic reasons why God had approved sex for married couples.

Firstly, because He desires that the earth is continually replenished. Recall that his maiden instruction to the first two human beings on earth had been; "Be fruitful and multiply, and replenish the earth, and subdue it" Gen1;28. Secondly, God prescribed marriage as in Genesis 2:24, and, therefore had approved sex for duly married couples so they might find sexual fulfillment even as they make themselves available for His special reward to man – children. The Psalmist said;

> *Lo, children are an heritage of the Lord: and the fruit of the womb is His reward. – Psalm 127:3.*

A third reason, which if you ask me I would say is the most important of all the reasons, why God had sanctioned marriage and approved sex for us you will find in His revelation through Prophet Malachi. After I read Malachi 2:15a, I realized that God doesn't just give children because He wants the earth replenished and filled, plus simply to bless families; but because, primarily, He is seeking godly offspring (seeds) He can use to advance His kingdom work on earth:

> *Has not the Lord made them one? In flesh and spirit*
> *they are His. And why one? Because He was seeking*
> *godly offspring (seed) KJV – Malachi 2:15a.*

Note that this scripture doesn't only enlighten us on the most fundamental reason God is ever inclined to sending children to bless families on earth. Reading this verse in between the lines, we will also observe that, because He is seeking godly offspring, God expects us to make spiritually conducive the condition around us before we ever commence the business of procreation. That is, we should endeavor to contract holy wedlock as the only acceptable platform for procreation.

At this point, I want to let us know some of those conditions which a Christian must rightly consider before commencing the business of procreation. But, before then I wish to quickly consider some procreation conditions God says are absolutely detestable to Him. Chapter Eighteen of the scriptures' book of Leviticus has a good record of several manners of sexual relations between any two human beings detestable to God. I believe God detests aberrant sexual relations because, quite obviously, any offspring from such unholy relationships can never turn out to be the godly offspring or seed He seeks.

You will recall that He had allowed David's son, the illegitimate product of his adulterous relationship with Bathsheba, Uriah's wife to die, 2 Samuel 12:18, and, yet, had granted the same woman the privilege of being the mother of David's son, Solomon, who succeeded him as king of Israel because they (David and Bathsheba) contracted a formal marriage later, after their adultery – 2 Samuel 11:27.

Human beings must realize that the ability to procreate is a very gracious right and, indeed, a privileged opportunity God gave to us to partake, so to say, in His divine work of creation. Observe that for a new human being to enter the world a man and woman must indulge in sexual intercourse for conception to occur; and afterwards the woman bears the child.

And we ought to realize too that the onus is on us, as parents, to endeavor to ensure that we do everything within our human capability to assist God in nurturing our children in the godly way. Unless we have the spiritual insight to raise them as godly children, our God will continue to count it as failure on our part. As parents, we have an obligation to help God raise godly seeds on earth. It is God's desire that every child born into the world, since after Jesus came to procure and secure salvation for the human race, be turned into a veritable seed for His use in uplifting His kingdom in the land. Hitherto Jesus, God had His own way of identifying His own godly seed in each of the past ages.

In Noah's age, for instance, it was Noah God had chosen to advance His work, He had used Noah to cleanse the earth of evil and everything unrighteous by flood. In another age, He had used Moses to liberate His people from captivity and oppression in a foreign land in Egypt.

Eventually, God had packaged His final and most precious gift to the entire world in the person of Jesus, His only begotten son, to release mankind from the oppression of the evil one, and to establish that sure highway for us to get to Him.

And now, because of Jesus' work of salvation, every child born into the world is a potential instrument, or a godly seed to be nurtured, for God's use in His work on earth. We must understand therefore that God gave us the gracious right, through His command in Genesis 1:28, to partake in the process of bringing children into the world because He expects that we should in no way be found to be lacking in the understanding that godliness should form that background in which they [children] must be raised.

Our God presumes we know that no godly seed or offspring can ever come from a sexual relation detestable to Him. Hear what He had told Moses as His ordinance to be relayed to the Israelites thus:

> *No one born of a forbidden marriage nor any of his descendants may enter the assembly of the Lord, even down to the tenth generation – Deuteronomy 23:2.*

The King James version of the Bible says, "A bastard shall not enter into the congregation of the Lord…." And the Oxford Advanced Learner's Dictionary (special price 7th edition) describes a bastard as a person whose parents were not married to each other when he or she was born.

Observe that God had handed down this injunction to the Israelites of old so that they might, amongst other things, be able to preserve the purity and honor of their families by excluding such as would be a disgrace to them. He gave the command as a check against whoredom in Israel, Deuteronomy 23:17.

If God wouldn't allow offspring from forbidden marriages, even amongst His chosen race, the Jews, be admitted into His holy congregation in the past; are we not supposed to know that He definitely expects us to meticulously keep this rule as well today? Our God doesn't ever change; He is the same God yesterday, today and forever – Hebrews 13:8.

Note These Offspring In The Scriptures Who Were Products Of Unholy Union That God Didn't Reckon With forever

Because God's ulterior motive for blessing or rewarding families on earth with children is so He might find godly seeds amongst them for His own use; then, it is out of place for anyone to imagine that any child from an unholy sexual relationship could ever be that seed God seeks.

Looking into the scriptures, I found some instances when God had truly rejected, or refused to reckon with, certain individuals because they were products of forbidden or illegitimate unions. One of such biblical personalities is Ishmael, you remember him? He was the product of Abraham's illicit relationship with his maidservant, Hagar. You will find the story in Genesis Chapter Sixteen.

The Bible records that Abraham had had this maidservant of his put in the family way because his bona fide wife, Sarah, was barren.

Hagar conceived and gave birth to a son who was named Ishmael. And, even though this child became Abraham's first son, yet, God didn't factor him in His scheme of things, but had chosen instead to wait for another son (Isaac) that was to be born by Sarah, Abraham's legitimate wife, according to his divine plan – See Genesis 17: 19-21.

God didn't accept Ishmael as His godly seed because he was a product of an illegitimate sexual relationship; exactly the same reason He did not allow king David's son from his adulterous sexual relationship with Bathsheba, Uriah's wife live. Both issues from these unholy unions couldn't have possibly been His desired godly seeds.

Granted, God is delighted when families are blessed with children, even as the earth is replenished and as people increase in number in the world. But, I could bet that God is more delighted in seeing these children raised as godly children (seeds). Because, according to Malachi, He needs as many godly children as possible in the land to do His divine work and uplift His kingdom on earth.

One benefit, parents must realize, which they stand to gain should they raise their children the godly way is that godly children can never be disobedient, nor rebellious. Disobedience, or rebellion, and other forms by which the recalcitrant trait is usually manifested by human beings, young or old, is a thing of the spirit. A godly child, one who has been duly cast upon God, John says, overcomes the spirit of the antichrist in the world; hear him thus:

Ye are of God, my little children, and have overcome them: because greater is he that is in you than he that is in the world. (1 John 4:4) KJV.

Joseph didn't ever show any bitterness towards his siblings even though they were jealous of him, and had hated him greatly for being their father's favorite child. And the Bible doesn't have any record of an act of waywardness, or disobedience, or rebellion that was perpetrated by Samuel even though he had been raised by a foster father whose own biological sons were notorious for their waywardness – 1 Samuel Chapter 2.

Before I close shop here in this chapter, let me at least mention a few rightful conditions that should form the foundation of any relationship between a man and a woman; the products of which God would delightfully accept as godly children (seeds).

Firstly, people must, as a matter of spiritual necessity, rightly determine when they are ripe enough to get into matrimony, and when to start bringing children into the world. Solomon the king of ancient Israel, who was a man full of abundant wisdom, had said that we shouldn't plant at will, and at any time, because there is a perfect time set by God in which to plant and reap bountifully – Ecclesiastes 3:2.

And, like I have said earlier in this chapter; DR. David Oyedepo says marriage (and in fact child-bearing) is not for boys and girls, but for young men and young ladies.

Secondly, people must arrange to be joined together as husband and wife in a holy wedlock before venturing into child-bearing. Unless, of course, a man and a woman have become husband and wife through a solemn union, any offspring they produce may never become a godly seed for

God's use. The end of the product of David's adulterous relationship with Bathsheba may well be remembered.

And finally, I think it is of utmost importance, as well as it is of much advantage, for persons getting into a marital relationship to first become born again. Jesus, in His teaching in Matthew 19 had taught the world heaven's rule of "One man, one wife." And in Genesis 2:24, we read that when a man marries a woman, the two become one flesh. Note that no two individuals (a man and his woman) can truly become one unless they are genuinely born again.

Observe that the bottom-line to this rule given by the Lord is that couples who get born again before marriage, and remain born again, are more likely to bear and rear their children as godly children (seeds)for God.

Chapter Three

Receive Every Child in the Lord's Name into Your Home

If only all families who do not know how to receive their new offspring into their fold would hear this: "if you understand the beginning well, the end will not trouble you." This is an African proverb I found very relevant and suitable to buttress my discourse in this chapter. And, besides this, the book of Ecclesiastes also taught that anyone who desires to reap abundant success in his work in the evening must endeavor to sow his seed properly in the morning (11:6).

No one knows the path of the wind, Solomon had said, or how the body is formed in a mother's womb. Just as no one can ever understand the work of our God, the maker of all things, see 11:5.

Having said this, let me quickly reiterate what I have said in the previous chapter, which is that God sends children to the world to bless and reward our human families; even as I ask whether families know how to nurture these precious gifts for God. Regrettably, most people do not realize that God expects them to have the requisite spiritual insight to be able to set their children on the path of godliness right from the word go as they arrive in the respective families in the world.

Friend, you need to hear some of the unimaginable things people do to these new babies when they receive them as gifts in their homes. And, these absurd practices, I must say, leave much to be desired from us by our God. I know that these ugly practices, from the very awkward ones to the absolutely pitiable ones, abound in the diverse cultures of the world. But, here, let me share a ridiculous story I heard from someone the other day with you.

Sometime ago, a friend of mine told me that in his community a new baby is seen, certainly, as a very precious and sacred gift from God. Sacred because they understand clearly that every child God sends to the world He had made in His own image and likeness. They know too that every baby born into the world has the fresh, uncontaminated spirit of God in it. And following this understanding, the people had established a custom to always dedicate their infant babies back to God.

But how do they do this dedication? No doubt you want to know. Now, according to my friend, every household in his community, customarily, owns a family shrine. And what they do is, any new baby born into a family is bathed first with water from a pot at the family shrine. And, then, the father of the new child must, as a matter of urgency, within 24 hours to be precise, "sow" (bury if you like) the placenta from the birth at the same family shrine.

Now, after this placenta is "sown" a stem (which is expected to grow into a tree) is planted on the particular spot for necessary identification; because every member of the family, old or young, male or female, is expected to own a tree at this shrine marking the spot on which his/her own placenta had been planted. When anyone dies, his/her tree is promptly felled.

I had found this story quite appalling. And I guess you will find it no less appalling too. My first impulse after I had heard this story was to think of these folks just like I had thought of the ancient Athenians who though had an inkling about a supreme deity who is the maker and the ruler of the entire world, but didn't have any idea how to reach out to that God, Acts 17: 22 -23. These folks, obviously, have the idea that new babies should be "sown" unto God, and within the family set- up at birth, but they simply lack the know-how to do it correctly.

Yes, it is right to sow our children as new members in our homes; but we must have the spiritual insight necessary to do so rightfully. Paul said you will reap exactly what you sow: when you sow to please your sinful nature, from that nature you will reap destruction; but when you sow to please the spirit, from the spirit you will reap eternal life –see Galatians 6:7b – 8.

Therefore anyone who dedicates his/her new baby to a family shrine like the folks above, or any god other than the Almighty God, is simply sowing to sinful nature. Observe that you only succeed in putting your child into a web for the enemy's manipulation and use when you dedicate it to a shrine – you sow the child to the sinful nature. Ecclesiastes 7:29 says;

> *God made mankind upright, but men have*
> *gone in search of many schemes.*

Peter had revealed in the scriptures that people conform to evil desires because they live in ignorance, 1 Peter 1:14. A lot of people cannot decipher and apply correctly God's principles in the scriptures meant to boost our Christian lives. For instance, many people, no doubt, know about Paul's revelation in the scripture quoted above; but regrettably, they do not seem to understand that this principle of sowing bountifully in order to reap bountifully relates to every area of our human endeavors or undertakings from which we expect God's reward.

Paul taught that to reap bountifully, you must first sow bountifully. This means, for instance, that if a laborer expects a bumper pay, he must endeavor to do some hard-work commensurate to his anticipated pay; just as a student who desires to pass his examination with flying colors must know what it means to burn the midnight oil.

An ancient philosopher once said; "Man was made free, but everywhere is in chain" What else does this mean other than that you put your child in chain when you dedicate it at a shrine. Human beings put themselves in chain, by and large, and indeed, actually limit their overall chances to succeed and prosper, by those bizarre things they do to, and with, themselves in life. God's blessings and prosperity for us are reserved only for those who are godly and obedient to His word. Understand therefore that when children are received (or sown) appropriately into our families at birth, they only but grow up to become godly adults available and eligible for God's blessings.

Observe that to sow, literally, means to plant or scatter (seed) for growth. Jesus in a parable in Mark 4:31-32, had likened a little child born into the world to a small mustard seed: He taught that the mustard seed is the smallest seed you plant in the ground; yet, when planted, it grows and becomes the largest of all garden plants, with such big branches that the birds of the air can perch in its shade.

Note that, in a similar vein, a newly born baby is the smallest form of the human being, and which when received (sown) appropriately in the name of the Lord into the family fold will grow up to become a great success to the delight of God Almighty. In other words, we always do have some planting (sowing) to do anytime we receive God's precious gift of a child in a home- this is what the Lord's philosophical teaching with the parable of the mustard seed above suggests.

And I believe that, apparently, my friend's folks I wrote about above do have this understanding. What I think they do not seem to have, however, is the spiritual insight to always sow or plant their children in the name of the Lord in their homes instead of at the shrines. Know that planting a newly born baby genuinely will require us to gratefully and thankfully receive the child into our family fold as God's special gift and reward for us, Psalm 127:3.

Then, we must present, and consecrate, the baby to the Lord in His vineyard (garden), so the child may be raised by the power of God Himself. Jesus was so presented and consecrated to God, see Luke 2:21. Planting in the Lord's vineyard is the second face of the entire planting process every baby must go through.

Note that whenever a child is born into any family, a new dream is born in that particular home. This birth of a new dream usually brings about the conception of a new desire for greatness and fulfillment in the hearts of all the family folks for the new member God has added to their fold. And this desire, usually, would trigger a quest for an assured life, a search for a definite pathway in which this child must tread to have his/her God-given destiny fulfilled. I am saying here that this all-important quest should always begin with a simple prayer, of this sort below, said to our God for the child by its parents. It is the surest foundation you could ever lay for your child:

Oh Lord God most high, we thank you for this precious gift of a child you have given to bless and reward us.

Your word, O God, says; "A man scatters seed on the ground. Night and day, whether he sleeps or gets up, the seed sprouts and grows, though he does not know how." Mark 4: 26b – 27.

Today, O Lord God, we lift up to you (should actually lift baby up here) this child you have given us as parents and have put in our care as its guardians.

We thankfully and gratefully accept this child into our home as one of us. Let this child grow up having your fear at heart and as a holy child in the land to the glory of your name. We pray in the name of JESUS CHRIST OF NAZARETH (AMEN).

You might be quick to take this prayer for granted. But, I must urge you to pause awhile and consider the Lord's teaching with the parable of the growing seed in Mark 4:26 – 30 quoted above. In a nutshell, this parable means that the best way to have an abundant harvest is to plant the seed, sleep and rise, and let the growth happen naturally. There is a guarantee here that God would cause the seed to produce bountifully; more so, if the planting (or sowing) was done in His name.

It is the same with the planting of your child I am talking about here. Note that a prayer, especially one said by a parent, for a child is a blessing. And, you know what! This sort of blessing is something more valuable than money, stronger than power, and deeper than any learning any child could ever acquire in life.

I have volunteered this short prayer as above because I have a passion to help God's people grasp the understanding that it is far more profitable to plant (or sow) our babies as new members in our homes; rather than to plant at demon shrines like my friend's folks I wrote about above. Or even to plant on a lake like Moses' mother had done, as we read in the scriptures – Exodus 2:3.

Now, let me make some very important issues out of the manner of planting Moses' mother had done with her little boy, Moses, as in the scriptures' verse mentioned above: What exactly was her reason for hiding her baby for 3 months initially, Exodus 2:2; and later, decided to "plant" or "sow" him on a lake? Shouldn't we, contemporary Christians, accept her reasons as good enough to stimulate us into doing some 'planting' for our children today?

First, the Bible records that Moses' parents had noticed that their baby, little Moses, was a fine child, Exodus 2:2, even as they had perceived that he was no ordinary child,

Hebrews 11:23. Therefore, by faith, they had hidden him for three months after he was born. And later, they had also had him planted on a lake, even when it meant defying the king's obnoxious edict, for maximum protection because they were desperate to save the child from being destroyed.

God's people should observe that the bottom-line for this action by Moses' parents was to have their little baby protected and saved from been killed by the enemy – the same reason why we should 'plant' our new babies in our homes, and later, in God's house today, as I will discuss shortly in the next chapter. Because, according to Peter, our enemy the devil prowls around like a roaring lion looking for someone (even infants at birth) to destroy – 1 Peter 5:8. The name of the Lord is a veritable weapon against his manipulation of our growing children.

I must also point out here from Moses' story mentioned above that, yes, his mother had had the initiative to hide and/or "plant" her little boy for God's protection from the enemy's antics. But beyond this, the woman, obviously, deserves some credit for having also had the foresight to help God raise her son as a godly seed: God used Moses to advance His kingdom's work greatly in the land.

Moses is still being remembered, till date, as the second greatest liberator of God's people; he's second only to the Savior, Jesus Himself. With the parable of the mustard seed, the Lord taught us that the seed, though usually very small, will often grow up to become the largest of all garden plants, Matthew 13:31 – 32. I guess this is provided, of course, that the seed was well sown on a fertile ground where it cannot be overwhelmed by weeds. To plant our children in Jesus' name is, no doubt, to plant in a very fertile ground.

To 'plant' or receive a new child into your home prayerfully in Jesus' name is tantamount to laying that solid foundation for God's overall blessing for the child. And, like I stated somewhere above, the genuine and proper "planting" of the new baby will only be complete and reasonable when the child is "planted" within Twenty-four hours of the its arrival in the home, and later, in God's house amongst His people on the eight day after birth – Let's discuss this in the next chapter.

Chapter Four

Dedicate Your Child to God

"Success for children doesn't just come; it's usually set in motion. My mother set mine in motion when she started by giving me bournvita Chocolate drink. Cadbury bounrvita drink is chocolate nourishment for tomorrow's leaders."

The above piece is an appeal to the buying public on bournvita chocolate drink running right now on our National television authority (NTA) here in Nigeria. The personality in this television advert is a young teenage girl. Now, see how you would like this same message when adapted for my Gospel Campaign thus:

"Godliness for children doesn't just come, it's usually set in motion. My parents set mine in motion when they had me cast upon Jesus in God's vineyard amongst God's people. Jesus is heaven's spiritual nourishment for tomorrow's leaders."

I am greatly fascinated by this, and I guess you are too. This piece is just about the summary of my entire message in this chapter. In the previous chapter I talked about receiving our new babies as fresh members into our families. And I did say that that was the first phase of the very necessary and important integration into the World Community our babies should be made to pass through.

Here, the second phase, as rightly suggested by the Chapter's caption, is that they should also be "planted" amongst God's people in His vineyard or house. To plant your child amongst God's people means to seek to connect the child to heaven. It means to practically hand-over your child to God for guidance, protection, and uplifting. Jesus had taught that the first assignment any human being on earth should endeavor to undertake is to seek to connect heaven for maximum prosperity and overall success – Matthew 6:33

And elsewhere in the scriptures, it's recorded that when people brought little children to Jesus to have Him touch (pray for) them, the disciples rebuked them, Mark 10:13. But when Jesus saw this, He was greatly indignant, and He promptly seized the occasion to teach His disciples, and, indeed, the whole world a very fundamental kingdom truth thus:

"Let the little children come to me, and do not hinder them, for the kingdom of God belongs to such as these.

I tell you the truth, anyone who will not receive the kingdom of God like a little child will never enter"- Mark 10:14 – 15.

Observe that flowing from this lesson by the Lord Jesus in these Bible verses above are the following basic truths:

1. Jesus is always available in God's genuine house to touch your child, but first, you must have the initiative to present the child to Him like the folks above did. "… Let the little children come to me," He had commanded.

2. The Lord revealed also that a human being is usually connected to heaven only as a baby; because in verse 15, He says; "anyone who will not receive the kingdom of God like a little child will never enter it." In other words, even you as an adult must change and become like a little child to be qualified to enter the kingdom of God – Obviously this is the concept behind being born again, John 3:3.

3. He says; "the kingdom of God belongs to children." When you present and consecrate your pure and innocent little child to God, the child becomes connected to heaven and every activity in the child's life, from infancy to adulthood, will come under the divine regulation and control of God Himself, see Matthew 11:25.

You got to understand, friend, that it's extremely important, and indeed expedient, for us to plant our children in God's vineyard amongst His people – to cast them upon Jesus the Lord for their protection and their ultimate success in life.

No doubt, you would remember David, the greatest king the ancient nation of Israel ever had. I got to know that the secret behind his overwhelming success during his reign over Israel was because he was cast upon God. He had revealed this in one of his very numerous songs of praise (the Psalms) he bequeathed to the world. Observe David's words thus:

> *From birth I was cast upon you; from my mother's*
> *womb you have been my God – Psalm 22:10.*

And in verse 9 of this same Psalm 22, David had also revealed that it was God who had practically taken charge of teaching him how to trust in, and rely on, Him absolutely at all times. This revelation by David here was, indeed, a hint as to the lesson, in Matthew 11:25 I have stated earlier, Jesus was to teach the world hundreds of years later.

The personal relationship David had with God was the reason he could survive the crises of a dozen lives during his time. You would recall that, somehow, he always bounced back from every trouble he ever encountered. And, somehow, he always maintained a passionate trust in God because apparently, he was connected to heaven.

Observe that David couldn't derail from the righteous path, no matter the odds that were against him and, in whatever awkward circumstance he ever found himself, because God was personally in charge of his life. In fact, David did demonstrate unusual love for God to the extent that he had earned His commendation as a man after His own heart from God Himself, Acts 13:22.

As a parent, you must understand that when your child is presented and consecrated to God, that is, cast upon Jesus in God's house, the child cannot be disobedient and rebellious; he cannot derail from the paths of righteousness and truth. David told us why in the scriptures thus:

> *My soul followeth hard after thee: thy right*
> *hand upholdeth me. (Psalm 63:8) KJV.*

David couldn't be heady when he was confronted over a crime as he naturally would have been, being king, because of his fear and love for God. He had simply let down his dignity as the highly respected king of Israel at Nathan's rebuke for killing Uriah after sleeping with Bathsheba, his wife. He had remorsefully admitted;" I have sinned against the Lord". See 2 Samuel 12:13

Note that David had been able to show this remorse for his sin only because his heart was following hard after God, having been cast upon Him. He knew for sure that God's right hand upheld him. Anyone cast upon God, unlike one who was not, invariably fears, regards, and respects God. Pharaoh, as you would recall, had had no fear, nor regards, for God; even in the face of the overwhelming miracles God had wrought to convince him to do His bidding as in the story of the liberation of the Israelites in the Scriptures.

Anyone cast upon God would never stop loving God; because it is God Himself who is in charge of his life. The wicked pride that is in the world cannot understand the kind of love for God I am talking about here. Observe what David, the man God had described as one after His own heart, had said in the scripture quoted earlier;" my soul followeth hard after thee".

And you know what friend! Following David's overwhelming love for God, God made sure his every step was always firm, though he stumbled many a time, He never allowed him to fall; He simply upheld him with his hand, Psalm 37:23-24. Apparently, David was not oblivious of the fact that he had God's love and help abiding for him; hence he had revealed that the secret to having such a blissful relationship with God was to;

Delight yourself in the Lord and He will give you the desires of your heart - Psalm 37:4.

Obviously, this wonderful revelation by David in this scripture verse above was the secret behind his victory, even as a teenager, over Goliath a renowned war champion, as recorded in 1 Samuel 17. Because David trusted God whole-heartedly, he knew that He always had his unflinching support for anyone who delights in Him; even in time of trouble. And so, he had had his confidence reposed in Him.

The scriptures say David had encouraged his folks not to loose heart over Goliath; while volunteering to go fight him even though he was the smallest Israelite present at that battle field, 1 Samuel 17: 32. David, no doubt, understood that Goliath, being a Philistine, wasn't circumcised, 1 Samuel 17: 26; and so was definitely not reckoned as one of God's people- see Genesis 17:14.

And for this reason he knew that his kinsmen only fretted because they did not understand that God does not save by sword or spear; for the battle is the Lord's. David understood that, because he delighted himself in the Lord, he was sure God would give him the desire of his heart- which was victory over Goliath and the Philistine's army, 1 Samuel 17:47. David, knowing that Goliath only terrorized and defied the armies of Israel to his peril, armed himself with only a string and five pebbles to square off against him. Hear David's boast to Goliath thus:

You come against me with sword and spear and javelin,
but I come against you in the name of the Lord Almighty,
the God of the armies of Israel whom you have defied...
Today ... the whole world will know that there
is a God in Israel. –1 Samuel 17:45-46.

And God didn't disappoint David either, for the victory indeed came for him – see verse 50. This victory came because David had learnt how to trust in, and rely absolutely on, God. Having been cast upon the Lord, he knew quite alright that a personal relationship existed between him and God. David had a remarkable understanding of the workings of God; and it's this understanding that made the difference here in his encounter with Goliath. It was this manner of understanding that also made Samuel stand out in his generation when he grew from an obscure background to become Israel's greatest leader ever.

I tell you something! A great deal of difference would always be made in the life of any child cast upon the Lord at birth: observe that even Moses whose mother had merely planted in water so he might not be destroyed by the wicked king of Egypt had been promoted remarkably to become second only to Jesus as liberator of His people.

Let me restate right now, for the avoidance of doubt and any ambiguity, those steps we should take as Christian parents to properly integrate our children into the world community so that they might grow up as godly children.

(1) Firstly, we must realize that children are God's precious gifts to us; and as such we should always receive them with much thanks to our God into our homes – see the prayer format I have offered in the previous chapter.

(2) Secondly, because the infant Jesus had been made to experience it on the eighth day after His birth, our male children must always be circumcised, see Luke 2 :21.

(3) And finally, our children must always be presented and consecrated to God so they might be under His divine care, guidance and protection. The Lord Jesus Himself was so presented and consecrated, see Luke 2:22-23.

Note that anyone not presented and consecrated to God (cast upon the Lord) may never experience the manifest presence of God in his/her entire life. But, God will always find a way to show up in the life of anyone who was formally made His own at infancy. The timing may be different for each individual, but, He sure always will.

Remember He showed up in Samuel's life when He called him as a little boy in 1 Samuel 3:4; God manifested Himself as fire over a bush in the desert when He came to commission Moses to liberate His people, the Israelites, from slavery in Egypt-Exodus 3. Moses was about forty years old then. What about David whom God had chosen as king over ancient Israel; whereas He had rejected his seven older siblings. David was only a teenager, and a mere sheep-tender then, 1 Samuel 16:12.

I guess I cannot help at this juncture, friend, but to urge you from the very bottom of my heart, to dare to present and consecrate your new baby to God and watch how He turns him/her into a huge success like the folks I've mentioned above.

Meanwhile, let me attempt to state some of the very numerous benefits of consecrating our children to God here as I round off this chapter:

(1) When a child is cast upon the Lord, the child's protection becomes God's responsibility absolutely. God will uphold the child with His own right hand, Psalm 63:8; He will care and protect the child, Night and Day; and make child "sprout" and "grow" whether the parents sleep or get up, like seed scattered on the ground, Mark 4:26-27. He had told David; "I will guide thee with mine eye." (Psalm 32:8) KJV.

(2) God always have a great life planned for any child consecrated to Him. See what He had said about the boy Samuel to the aged Priest Eli, his foster father, thus:

*I will raise up for myself a faithful priest, who will
do according to what is in my heart and mind.
I will firmly establish his house, and he will minister
before my anointed one always - 1 Samuel2:35.*

(3) The child will grow, and wax strong in spirit, he will be filled with wisdom: and the grace of God will be upon him, Luke 2:40 (KJV).

(4) Such a child will, no doubt, grow up to become a godly seed (child) in God's hand, doing God's work; see Jesus' statement in Luke 2:49 (KJV). Remember, even Moses who was only informally cast upon the Lord, because he was "planted" on a lake, ultimately fulfilled his God-given destiny although he had strayed at the outset of his life.

(5) A child who belongs to God hears what God says always, that is, would always obey God's commands. He cannot be disobedient and rebellious, John 8: 47.

(6) A child dedicated to God automatically becomes one of Jesus' sheep; and only Jesus' voice will he/she ever know because He (Jesus) promptly becomes his/her Shepherd. In fact, the scriptures say the child will never follow a stranger (the devil), he will always run away from him because he won't ever be able to recognize his voice – see John 10:4 – 5.

(7) Any child consecrated to God begins to receive vital lessons from God on how to trust in, and rely on, Him at all times and in all situations, starting from its mother's breast – Psalm 22:9.

(8) And finally, any child presented and consecrated to
God would have more insight about God's word than
even all his teachers, Psalm 119:99, more understanding
than the elders, verse 100, and this is because God
Himself will become the child's teacher – See verse
102. Obverse here that David had only acknowledged
God's faithfulness to the promise He had made to him
in Psalm 32:8; when He said, "I will instruct you and
teach you in the way you should go. I will counsel you."

We read in the scriptures that Jesus started demonstrating
unmatchable insight and understanding of God's word over
and above his peers, and even the elders He ever came across,
at the tender age of twelve.

Luke Chapter two verse forty-six records that when His
parents eventually found Him, following His disappearance
around the temple for three days during a particular Passover
feast, He was sitting among some great teachers; listening
to them and asking them questions. And verse 47, says;
"Everyone who heard him was amazed at His understanding
and His answers."

Chapter Five

Ensure Your Child is Decently Socialized

Socialization is a fundamental duty which the world owes every child born into it. Because, through the study of psychology, it has been ascertained that every new baby into the world always comes with a "tabula-rasa mind"--one with no pre-established ideas, thoughts, and reasoning abilities.

Therefore, every child born into the world will not be able to function as a rational member of the society, unless and until, he/she is adequately socialized by the various agencies of socialization as identified by the sociologist; namely:

1. The home or family
2. The church
3. The school
4. The media
5. The child's peer group.
6. Others

Before I proceed to discuss the inputs each of these agencies needs to make towards the overall development of a child, I wish to earmark very quickly here that, even though we have multitudes of these agencies in our societies right now, they just do not seem to be up to much success because they do not really bother to make holiness and righteousness their watchwords.

Solomon had revealed that the whole duty of man (every human being) in the world is to revere God and keep His commandments always, Ecclesiastes 12:13. In view of this, teachers in the respective socializing agencies I have highlighted above would do better if they could always consciously make godliness the bottom-line of their lessons to growing children in order that they might grow up to become godly, obedient and responsible members of our societies.

Here, let us see some of the issues each of these afore-mentioned socializing agencies should teach to our children:

1. The Home or Family

A child's parents, plus its immediate family members constitute the first unit of the society every new baby born into the world always gets to interact with; and so, be socialized by.

It is the duty of all members of a child's family, especially the parents, to teach a child the basic lessons of life. A child who has been well tutored by its parents cum immediate family members on how to obey rules and regulations, to be respectful or truthful, etc; will definitely not be found wanting in character nor in morality out there because of the lessons he has learnt at the home front.

Parents must realize that they owe it as a parental obligation to teach their children the word of God and to set them on the path of righteousness so they can live all the days of their lives for God. This is one of the reasons I had mentioned spiritual maturity as a necessary pre-condition for marriage in chapter one. Because, when a child's parents are not born again, and so, not spiritually mature before marriage, there is no way they would be able to meet the spiritual needs of their offspring. It is only when a child lives in a home where godly virtues such as love, respectfulness, righteousness, truthfulness, etc, are esteemed that he/she learns to show love to others; and be respectful, righteous, truthful, in his daily dealings with others as well.

Observe, friend, that the very high level of ungodliness and moral bankruptcy in our world community today is owing to the prevalence of multitudes of parents out there who are, themselves, not upright in their ways, and so, cannot in anyway groom their children to be morally and religiously upright. I think it is a big shame, especially for professed Christians; because our God is not happy with this ugly situation.

2. The Church

The church as an agency for socialization charged with the responsibility to enlighten people generally, and children in particular, on the word and ways of God, do not seem to be living up to her responsibilities these days. A radio commentator on Christianity who couldn't hide his feelings about this situation said the other day that; "we have a million and one churches these days, but quite unfortunately, not one of them could be trusted as being able to lead anyone to salvation".

I couldn't help but agree absolutely with this preacher when I heard this statement which actually derogates the generality of preachers. This is because his observation, to a very large extent, is just not deniable. Instead of preaching salvation for God's people, the key sermon our preachers preach from the pulpits in our churches of today has become solely prosperity.

Meanwhile, it is undeniably the duty or responsibility of the church to cater for the spiritual needs of our children and, indeed, all God's people in the world. That the church owes it as its duty to teach to everyone born into the world God's acceptable ways to salvation;and thereby, to make sure that no soul is destroyed by the enemy is simply not questionable.

It is in the light of this that every preacher of God's word should always see himself as an agent of God whose job is, oftentimes an all- encompassing one. He must understand that, in contrast to other professionals who specialize, as a preacher, he will always be required to call upon wide-ranging skills in helping God's people.

For instance, depending on the given situation he finds himself, a preacher may act, as a psychologist, a sociologist, a social worker, an administrator, personnel supervisor, philosopher and, indeed, as a communicator.

Many people do not realize that what God had used His servant, Jonah, to do in the lives of the Ninevites, according to the story in Jonah Chapter 3, was to socialize, civilize and promote them. Because to socialize, as a matter of fact, means enlightening someone (or a people) so that he/she can get promoted by God from a condition of no benefit to that of much benefits. So that he or she can be lifted from grass to abundant grace.

Preachers, therefore, are supposed to be God's own agents for socializing and civilizing His people on earth. Observe how Jonah's preaching to the Ninevites had had a civilizing influence on them. Jonah 3:10 records that at Jonah's preaching, the people had turned from their evil ways, and this made God to look on them with compassion, and so, did not bring upon them the destruction he had threatened.

3. The School

The school, as rightly identified by the sociologists, is an indispensable agency or institution for the socialization of children (and people generally) in any community. School teachers and administrators must therefore realize that the community, and indeed God, expects them to strive always to complement the effort of a child's parents at home, as well as that of the church in order to achieve the best overall development of a child. Granted, the basic function of the school in a given society is usually to meet the academic needs of people. But, beyond this, I think it definitely would do communities a world of good if issues relating to godliness, and the worship of God, are usually factored into our children's schooling curricula.

Because, by and large, the sum of the reasons why God makes human beings on earth, according to Solomon in Ecclesiastes 12:13, is that we might fear Him and obey His commandments – this is the whole duty of man on earth. We therefore must always feel challenged to meet with our God's standards for us in everything we do, even with schooling.

It is simply not enough to have a child study a course in engineering, or in business, or in humanities etc, without inculcating in him sound moral and godly values. Education without God is nothing but absolutely valueless. In Matthew 23:23, the Lord Jesus had rebuked the teachers of the law and the Pharisees for neglecting more important matters of the law (matters of God, because Jesus who fulfilled the law is God).

And there He had identified these more important matters of God to include; justice, mercy and faithfulness as against other less important matters they usually strove to keep. And what does it matter actually if a child is made to acquire all the academic education there is in the world, but the child has no fear of God? – Matthew 16:26.

4. The Media

The media has also been identified by the sociologists, as an agency for socialization in the community. But, the activities of this agency, as everyone on the side of righteous living would have observed, are now so tilted towards secularity that one is almost absolutely correct to say that our media outlets are doing more harm than good to people in the society today, especially our children.

And the irony is that, no one seems to be showing any concern about the negative impact this agency is having on people in the world right now. I guess, however, that it is because people do not realize the magnitude of the influence media homes could have on their growing children.

The other day, a friend of mine told me a little story of how his 3-year-old boy had cried for hours on end in reaction to a TV promo on a particular food-seasoning product. My friend said the marketing company's appeal to the buying public that had been shown on the screen had featured several people who ate several plates of rice that were well garnished with chicken meat.

Now, he said after his boy had keenly watched these TV personalities devour this mouth-whetting food completely; he got upset and cried profusely. The little boy couldn't help but complain to his parents that his reason for crying was, because; as he had said it "the people inside the television didn't give me rice." Quite ridiculous, you might say! But I tell you, this is exactly how great the power or influence is that the media could have on our children.

Here, let me advice two material groups who could be counted upon to stem this ugly trend towards secularity by the media; they are our earthly parents and the media regulatory bodies cum government.

Our parents must realize that it is part of their parental obligations to their kids to monitor the programs they watch on the television. That, it is their duty to restrict growing children from reading materials which are capable of leaving negative thoughts and ideas on their minds.

Know that there is nothing wrong if, as a parent, you decide to copy out all the enlightening and entertaining children's programs on the TV on paper, have it hung somewhere in the home for the childrenwith an instruction that they mustn't watch any program not on that list on TV. Let your children know that obedience to dad or mum's instruction is of essence; because your wish is to have them grow into God-fearing, obedient, and responsible adults.

And on the part of the Government, I think that each national Government should, through the regulatory bodies set up by them, always seek to monitor activities of the media houses, both electronic and print, in order to check their excesses. People in government must realize that it is purely their responsibility to encourage legislation against the airing, and /or the printing of materials capable of negatively affecting our children's moral and spiritual bearing.

5. The Peer Group

Our children's playmates, whether in our neighborhoods, or at the various schools they attend, constitute one large informal group that wields enormous power to influence our growing children. But, unfortunately, most of our parents have always failed to recognize this group.

Paul had taught believers in 1 Corinthians 15:33, that bad company corrupts good character, "And he had gone further to teach that believers do not have any reason to have themselves yoked with unbelievers, 2 Cor 6: 14; even as he had asked the following rhetorical questions:

For what do righteousness and wickedness have in common? Or what fellowship can light have with darkness?

What harmony is there between Christ and Belial? What does a believer have in common with an unbeliever?

What agreement is there between the temple
of God and idols?- 2 Cor, 6:14b – 16a.

Christian parents should understand that as believers, they, and their children, are symbols of God's righteousness and light in the world. They should understand that they constitute the temple of the living God on earth, verse 16b.

Having said this, I must inform our parents that it is their duty to monitor the caliber of persons their children befriend and those they hang out with as friends. Granted that children are, by their nature, and perhaps, because of the fear of being spanked by mummy or daddy, usually given to being discreet in their dealings. Most children would feel freer with their classmates and playmates than they would with their parents at home, with teachers at schools, and even, with the pastor at the church.

Parents should always endeavor to break every peer group jinx on their children by being very close to them. They should, as much as possible, make sure their children learn most of the fundamental truths they need to know about life first hand from them. Note that unless you teach your children with love some basic truths about life, particularly about the worship of God, your children will have no choice other than to pick up wrong ideas from their peers and others outside.

I must state unequivocally that I am not in anyway insinuating that our children should not be permitted to keep friends. I am only advocating that believers should teach and encourage their children to pick and befriend other responsible children out there whose friendship will not interfere with their godly walk.

I read in the scriptures' book of 1 Samuel chapter 20, how Jonathan, Saul's son, had helped David to escape from being killed by his father, even at his own detriment. Observe that David would probably not have fulfilled his God-given destiny; that is, to be king over Israel, if he hadn't found true and genuine friendship in Jonathan.

Theirs was friendship for a common goal, which was to actualize God's plan for David's life – that is, to promote God's work on earth. Till date, their loyalty and love still make for one of the most beautiful stories of friendship ever told.

This is the kind of friendship our children should be taught to emulate. Parents should endeavor to let their children know that friendship with the world can never be for the best interest of believers. Many who call themselves your friends would prefer to join the rest of the world in walking out on you, rather than walk in, when you need them most. Some would just be fair weather friends, and still, others would not hesitate to tear you down at any slight opportunity.

6. Others

Under this group, I would like to mention several other organizations such as rehab homes (or reformation homes as they are called in some countries), Christian training / counseling organizations, Unicef children's department etc.

It is my belief that if people who may find themselves as workers in these various organizations usually saddled with children's concerns make the word of God the fundamental tool their job they certainly would always be in for great success.

You would agree with me that the essence of having to rehabilitate or reform a growing child or an individual is so that he/she can eschew his/her delinquent tendencies. In other words, rehabilitation or reformation is synonymous with molding in a sense. And the Scriptures say, according to the Apostle Paul, that the best tool available for achieving much success in the undertaking of molding a human being is God's word; hear him thus:

> *"All Scriptures is God breathed, and is useful for teaching, rebuking, correcting and training in righteousness, so that the man{child} of God may be thoroughly equipped for every good work.*
>
> *2 Timothy 3: 16—17.*

Now, if Paul, a most renowned new testament preacher had taught this; then, there is simply not much anyone else can say anymore about the word of God being the most effective tool for correcting the growing children under our care as reasonable adults in the society

I rest my case here, in so far as Paul's teaching in the Scripture quoted above has suitably, and unambiguously, summed up my point.

Chapter Six

Never Refrain From Punishing Your Child When He Errs

Everyone familiar with pottery would readily remember and, no doubt, agree with me here that the potter's job is usually done in stages: from sourcing his clay, which is his major material, to having the finished product in his hands ready for the market, the potter must work through the following processes or stages:

1. First, he sources his material, clay.
2. Then, he must sieve and mix clay into a smooth and moldable pastry form.
3. Next, he molds clay into his desired shapes and sizes.
4. And then, he designs the molded products.
5. After which, the products are subjected to heat in an oven, that is, they are "baked" to make them solid and strong. And finally, the finished products are polished, and made ready for the market.

These are the basic stages any product made of clay would have gone through before becoming a usable item in the hand of the end user.

Now, quite similarly, every one born into the world does have three stages of life to live in from infancy to adulthood; and these are; the childhood stage, adolescent stage, and finally, the adult stage. Childhood is that period of a human being's life when he/she is still a child, the adolescent stage is the period when a child has developed into a young adult, and it's always between the age of twelve and eighteen. And the adult stage is that stage at which a person becomes fully grown and capable of taking actions for which he/she will be legally responsible.

Observe, therefore, that flowing from the above definitions; a child is simply a young human being who, though not unthinking, but, is not always capable of making any rational or productive decision without assistance. But, does this basic fact form part of the knowledge parents out there hold about their children in order that they might raise them properly?

Unarguably, many of our parents do not realize that a child in its childhood period is only but a child. They do not realize that the nature of handling a child requires during childhood is not the same as what is required to care for the young human being during the adolescent stage.

If only our parents would ever pause to reflect on the reason why children are never allowed to administer medicines all by themselves; as the inscription, "keep out of reach of children", is usually written on packages of medicines, but adults are never included in this group barred from this drug use? It is because they {children} are not always capable of taking rational decisions, and so to give a child the free hand to administer a drug all by himself is to provide him an opportunity to abuse the drugs.

A kingdom truth I must sell to you here is that; you must collaborate with God in any aspect of your life in which you desire to achieve success. And no one can collaborate with God effectively unless, and of course, he understands that God always does His work according to a pre- planned order: He is a God who is ever given to perfect orderliness.

The story of creation in the scriptures' book of Genesis, chapter one to be precise, readily gives credence to this statement of mine here. That is, that, indeed, God's work is usually done through a process, and according to His plan. Here, let me show you, from the scriptures, one great promise God had made to David, a man whom He later described as one after His own heart, Acts 13:22, because, I like to use it as a premise for further discussion here in this chapter. Hear this:

I will instruct you and teach you in the way you should go; I will counsel you and watch over you - Psalm 32:8.

Observe that we have in this great promise the following key words;

1) Instruct
2) Teach
3) Counsel
4) And, watch (or guide as in KJV)

We must understand that our God is ever wiling to undertake the task of watching over anyone who is His own throughout his lifetime; and to instruct, teach, and counsel those who endeavor to walk His righteous paths in each of the three stages of their lives. God never leaves one who is His own alone, neither does He ever forsake him, Deut 31:6.

It is apparent, from the foregoing paragraph, that the specific areas in which a parent is required to collaborate with God while raising a child in the godly way will include; instructing the child, teaching the child, counseling, and watching or guiding the growing child. Note, however, that while a parent's obligation to his offspring in all these respects is simply terrestrial in nature, God's own control or regulation of the child's life is by supernatural influence.

Having said this, let me again restate here what I said about the potter and his job above: Now, the Potter's most fundamental job after he must have sourced his material, which is clay, and has sieved and mixed the clay, is to mold it into his desired shapes or figures. You must observe that everything else the potter would do to his molded figure from this point on would simply be directed at making it strong and appealing as a usable item eventually in the hands of the user.

Parents therefore need to understand that a new baby into their homes does require some molding before being "baked" and, then, "polished" to turn the child into a refined and well-groomed adult for God's use, and for the betterment of the society. The potter, every one conversant with one would recollect, is a very meticulous worker whose watchword in his trade is usually excellence.

In a similar vein, therefore, parents who desire to raise their children as godly children who would make great success out of their lives must realize that the childhood stage is of utmost consequence. It is one stage that is synonymous with the molding stage in the pottery trade; and parents should endeavor to be stern and always very decisive in their dealings with their children during this stage. Any parent worth his salt must be able to discipline his child for any act of naughtiness; and be able to master very firmly every tendency in the child to be unruly in his/her behavior.

There is nothing wrong in going beyond merely scolding a child when he misbehaves; you could spank your child sometimes in addition to scolding. A child in this childhood stage usually requires very firm handling. Note, however, that whenever the need arises for you to scold and/or spank your child, it should always be followed by a counseling session in which you are required to offer the child very sound, intelligent and faultless advice. And the bottom-line must be God's word.

You must also realize that it is of utmost importance to always make the child know or understand the particular offence for which he has been punished; and to tell him how to avoid having to commit a similar one in future.

The childhood stage, if I may reiterate, is the molding stage for the child; and you would recall, as I have said earlier also, that the molding stage is the most tasking in all the stages a potter always gets to work through: and this is why the potter can not help but be very rugged while molding and beating the clay into his desired structures or shapes. His resourcefulness in the areas of design and polishing only go to add beauty to the already well-molded structures.

"No one can bend a dried fish "so a common saying always goes. And the author of Hebrews says; "No discipline ever does seem pleasant at the time, but painful. Later on, however, it produces a harvest of righteousness and peace for those who have been trained by it" – Hebrews 12:11. Your child during his childhood stage needs to be handled with iron hands, Solomon says parents who won't discipline their children are in danger of ruining them, Proverbs 29:15. And in so many other verses in the book of Proverbs he had taught about the danger of not adequately exercising control over our children. See some as follows:

He who spares the rod hates his son, but he who loves him is careful to discipline him – Proverbs 13:24.

Discipline your son, for in that there is hope; do not be a willing party to his death. – 19:18.

Folly is bound up in the heart of a child, but the rod of discipline will drive it far from him 22:15.

Do not withhold discipline from a child; if you punish him with a rod, he will not die. Punish him with the rod and save his soul from death – 23: 13- 14.

Discipline your son, and he will give you peace he will bring delight to your soul 29: 17.

God expects that every parent is able to reasonably control his children. He expects parents to be firm and always very decisive in meting out punishment on their children whenever the need arises. I believe Solomon caught this revelation absolutely hence he had devoted a considerable part of the Bible's book of proverbs to his teachings on this very critical subject of children upbringing.

Proper children upbringing, as we must observe, is an issue our God feels very much passionate about. Every Bible scholar would, no doubt, readily remember how He had punished, without hesitation, an aged priest named Eli who worked at Shiloh for failing in his fatherly obligation to control and discipline his wayward children appropriately; See 1 Samuel 2:30 – 36.

Priest Eli, according to this Bible account, had simply lacked the audacity to adequately check his children's misdemeanor. As a result of this, God said he honored his Sons more than Him 1 Samuel 2:29. Eli couldn't hide under the guise of being ignorant of their misbehavior, because first Samuel 3:13 says he had known about his sons' disgraceful behavior in the tabernacle of God, and even though he had rebuked them, he earned God's wrath because he had "failed to restrain them" appropriately. This is exactly what majority of our parents do today. I must tell you that it is always a surprise to me anytime I witness or experience a situation where a parent gets unnecessarily complacent with his/her child or ward who misbehaves.

I think people must realize, like Solomon did, that for any parent, especially one who is a professed Christian, to fail in his God-given task of rearing his child properly is to earn God's sanction. It was for no less a reason that Solomon had thought it wise to assist God's people in this regard by leaving a body of lessons for our use in this contemporary times. The book of Proverbs in the Bible is replete with these lessons. I have already quoted some of them above; you will do well to visit this book for more doses of his instructions on this subject matter.

It is often said that charity begins at home; I must let you know also that the recalcitrant attitude usually begins to form in the child at home. If what a child usually gets for being naughty and disobedient at home is a mere rebuke without a commensurate punishment for his offence; then there is no telling that the child will go out and not be disrespectful to teachers at school, or be insubordinate at the work place when he grows up.

Compromise on moral and behavioral laxity is a weakness which most parents around the world exhibit these days, and this I strongly feel is the cause of the high attitudinal rot our children display in the societies today. Most parents simply think that to thrash a child for wrongdoing is not to show love to the child. Whereas, Solomon had revealed that it is only out of profound love that a parent must discipline a child who commits an offence. See what he said thus:

> *My son, do not despise the Lord's discipline*
> *and do not resent his rebuke, because the Lord*
> *disciplines those He loves, as a father the son*
> *he delights in – Proverbs 3: 11 – 12.*

I do not think that Solomon is here in this verses advocating excessive or overbearing oppression of a child in the name of discipline, as some parents would do owing to frustration. But that parents should learn to always mete out punishments reasonably to their children whenever they err, or become unruly was king Solomon's take on this issue.

This reminds me of a little advice I rendered to a lady friend of mine sometime ago. This woman had complained bitterly about how it had become practically difficult for her to curtail her 16-year- old daughter's behavioral excesses. She told me that this daughter of hers used to be a fascinating young girl, one who was always amiably disposed to everyone until she became twelve and suddenly began to change. "Didn't the scriptures teach that a parent who spares the rod hates his/her child? Ever since my daughter was a child I have never ceased wielding the cane to carefully discipline her anytime she committed an offence because I love her so much, Proverbs 13:24. Where could she have picked her unruly behavior? Even the cane no longer has any effect on her, she now practically wrestles with me anytime I wield the cane these days," the woman had agonized.

Diagnosing what the problem was between this woman and this errant daughter of hers was quite easy. On the one hand, I understood that the young girl had come of age and had began to feel as though she were already an adult. And on the other hand, I was able to fathom that this woman had failed to realize that the manner of punishment or disciplinary measure to be meted out to a child for being unruly ought to be varied according to the age and/or maturity of the child.

In helping this particular woman restore her soured relationship with her daughter, I had informed her of the need to alter a child's punishment for offences committed as he/she grows up in this manner I have stated below. I guess this could be of immense benefit to many people out there; hence, I have formatted everything I had told this woman here. I have offered this as a mere pointer to how we should endeavor to mold and train our children while they grow up.

Age	Suggested Suitable Treatment
2 – 6 years	Teach child by showing example. Children under this age bracket learn mainly by copying or mimicking what they see or hear. Nothing wrong with spanking the child when he/she does something wrong.
7 – 12 years	Children while within this age bracket could be given some strokes of the cane when they go wrong. Give them instructions and ensure they carry them out. Teach them by showing example, even as you always endeavor to give them oral teaching, especially on the word of God. You could also punish them by asking them to kneel down, do some domestic work, refuse them permission to watch TV, play Video games, etc.
13 – 18 years	A child within this age bracket would definitely have started experiencing those signs that herald adulthood, e.g. development of the reproductive organs. Here, adequate care must be employed in handling the child. Parents should endeavor to instruct, teach and counsel the young person un-relentlessly. You could ground, ask child to kneel, or make the child do some domestic work as punishment when he/she commits an offence.
Young Adults above 18 years of age	Our children, who have attained this age, are nothing but young adults who should be wisely and intelligently helped to land safely on the spectrum of adulthood. We must therefore endeavor not to loose steam on our efforts at instructing, teaching and giving them good counsel on the word of God – which is the only true way in life. Merely rebuking your child who has become a young adult would always do when he/she commits an offence. Counseling becomes your most fundamental obligation to your child here. Titus 2:6 – 8a might be of immense assistance here.

At this juncture, I would like to offer you some additional very useful hints to help you become better in the parenting of your children. But before I do that, I wish to quickly let you know that after I had spoken with the woman I mentioned above, she got back to me some weeks later to thank me for my assistance. Baring her mind, she had told me that she had simply adopted counseling as a tool to solve the problem of checking her daughter's misbehaviors. She actually told me of a particular counseling session she had had one night with her usually errant daughter, and how the young lady had been broken with deep emotions of guilt, and she had begged remorsefully for forgiveness. "Your advice worked"! The woman had exclaimed with great excitement.

I was really glad that I could help this woman. And because my desire, also, is to be able to help thousands of people out there in raising their children according to our God's standards; I thought it wise to leave these (7) hints for better parenting below for you:

1. Always seek good and/or godly advice concerning your children's life. As a parent you should endeavor to emulate Samson's father, Manoah, in the scriptures, see Judges 13:12.
2. Let the atmosphere around your home be filled with love all the time. Parents should understand it as their duty to create a loving home. Paul taught that it is a continuing debt for family members (and all human beings) to love one another, Romans 13:8.
3. Parents must have the audacity to exercise their parental authority always at the home front. And

the child, the Bible teaches, ought to obey their parents in everything because it pleases the Lord Colossians 3:20, and, according to Moses' law, so that it might be well with them Exodus 20:12.1 also read in my Bible that every father{parent}has heaven's unlimited authority and permission to discipline his son-see Hebrews 12:7. And the author also went ahead to reveal that any son or child not always disciplined by his father is better considered not as a true son, but an illegitimate child- verse 8; and he taught that respect and much regards are what a child owes a father who consciously disciplines him-verse 9.

4. Parents must define family rules and always endeavor to enforce them promptly.

5. Ensure that you establish and maintain daily routine for the children.

6. Our children whether at, infancy or childhood, or at adolescent, and at the young adult, stages are human beings who have their feelings to express too. Parents should always endeavor to acknowledge their children's feelings. Paul admonished parents not to embitter their children so that they do not become discouraged – See Colossians 3:21.

7. Every parent should learn to teach and lead his/her child by example. I read in one of John Maxwell's book titled; "THE POWER OF THINKING BIG" that people are usually changed, not by coercion or intimidation, but by example.

And Titus 2:6-8 says believers (and indeed all parents) must learn to encourage their young adult-children: In everything set them an example by doing what is good.

In teaching your children, you must show integrity, seriousness and soundness of speech that cannot be condemned; so that the children may never have anything bad to copy from you.

Chapter Seven

God Helps in Raising His Own

Somewhere previously in this book, I have mentioned that God delights greatly in having people work with Him towards the attainment of His divine goals in our lives, and on earth. But regrettably, the world knows nothing about this very viable heaven's principle. As a result of this, many people, including believers, have always failed to excel in many departments of their lives, even at raising godly children.

Let me share with you a verse from the scriptures that I found tucked neatly into one of David's songs of praise, the Psalms, and which reveals exactly what God actually expects us to do to our children. It is only when we understand and work along these lines that He will also work to complement our efforts at raising our children as the godly seeds He seeks for His kingdom work in the land. See this;

I will instruct thee and teach that in the way which thou shalt go: I will guide thee with mine eye - Psalm 32:8.

Every parent who is a believer has the right to take the words of Psalm 32: 8 quoted above as though they were written just for himself and his children; because they are indeed, God's promise to every child born into the world: Especially those cast upon Him, as David was, at birth.

Observe what God had promised David here, by paying particular attention to the underlined words, He says; "I will instruct thee and teach thee in the way which thou shalt go: I will guide thee with mine eye". Apparently, an individual pathway is here promised David by God as distinguished from the general way of righteousness set before all Christians to follow.

The three words used by God here in telling us how exactly He expects earthly parents to collaborate with Him in raising their children are; instruction, teaching and guidance.

These are God's matchless words to us promising His partnership with earthly parents in the business of molding the children He sends to them as godly children in the world. Believers ought to understand therefore that they must cooperate with God in His divine program of making godly seeds out of their children; "for we are God's fellow workers", See 1 Corinthians 3:9.

Note that the word instruct, or instruction, within the context of its celestial usage here means "the enlightening of the intelligence. While "teaching" is the pointing out of a definite course. "Guidance" means the advice needed for particular problems. And to "control", which is another tool God may decide to use sometimes, as suggested in Psalm 32:9, means to enforce obedience.

Observe that God is telling us in Psalm 32:8 that He is ever ready to do all these in our lives as believers, and especially in our growing children's lives; more so, when we have them cast upon Him. His delight and, indeed, passion is in seeing that, according to Prophet Malachi in 2:15, all the children He sends to the world are raised as godly children (seeds).

Now, I believe God had given these words through David to us because of our ignorance. God knows that, unless He enlightens us on how exactly to rear our children, His finding godly seeds on earth might just be a mirage. This had been expressed by David in the scriptures in his prayer in Psalm 12:1 thus:

Help, Lord; for the godly man ceaseth; for the faithful fail from among the children of men. – (Psalm 12:1) KJV

And the Lord Jesus Christ Himself didn't withhold heaven's reservation regarding this issue of finding godly children in the world at His return, hence He had said;

"…. However, when the son of men comes will he find faith on the earth?" - Luke 18:8.

I must tell you that this might pretty well be one of the reasons God hadn't let anyone, not even His beloved son, nor the angels, know the day or hour when Jesus shall return, Mark 13:32. God expects that we learn and know the ropes regarding how to raise our children the godly way. And He is thus ever prepared to wait very patiently for as long as it would take Christians to aid Him in realizing

His goal of finding godly children on earth. The Psalmist reveals that God's search for a godly seed on earth, which has transcended many generations, continues thus:

God looks down from heaven on the sons of men to see if there are any who understand, any who seek God. - Psalm 53:2.

Do you know, friend, that God wouldn't have destroyed Sodom and Gomorrah if He had found just a single godly individual out there in either of the cities? See His little chat with Abraham, (His friend) that had preceded the destruction of these two ancient cities in Genesis chapter 18.

But, unlike Sodom and Gomorrah; Nineveh, which used to be one of the largest and most important cities in the then Assyria, had been lucky; God had found His servant, Jonah, who was a prophet in Israel, whom He sent as His godly seed to preach against their evil deeds. And the Bible records in Jonah 3:10, that at Jonah's preaching, the Nenevites had repented of their sins; and thus, God had had compassion and did not bring upon them the destruction He had threatened.

Let me pause briefly to answer two very critical questions here, which are indeed relevant to the issue under focus; "How can a young man keep his way pure," this a question the Psalmist had asked in Psalm 119:9; and closely related to this, let me also ask here right now, "what must we teach to our children, or instruct them on, as we collaborate with God in raising them as godly seed?

When you read Psalm 119:9 closely, you would observe that the Psalmist had done well to provide an answer to his own question; he had revealed that, it is by living according to God's word. No doubt, the Psalmist's answer here is also a suitable answer to my second question asked above.

What all parents must endeavor to teach their children, and instruct them on, are the tenets for righteous living as prescribed in the scriptures. Note that God's word is the only sure key to living a genuinely prosperous life. No wonder Moses had unequivocally counseled the Israelites, in the Old Testament era, on the need to teach God's word to their children always thus:

These commandments (God's word) that I give you today are to be upon your heats. Impress them on your children.

Talk about them when you sit at home and when you walk along the road, when you lie down and when you get up.

Tie them as symbols on your hands and bind them on your foreheads. Write them on the doorframes of your houses and on your gates - Deuteronomy 6:6-9.

Believers should understand that God's instruction, and teaching to human beings is usually by impartation through the spirit on our minds and/or souls. But, so that understanding might be adequately gained by the children we rear, in Proverbs 4:1, Solomon the wisest amongst all men who have ever lived on the surface of the earth, taught that it is a father's duty to instruct his child, and a mother's to teach the child, every good lesson there is about life, and the word of God, a child needs to learn – See Proverbs 1:8 and 6:20.

And, in 2 Timothy 3: 16, Paul had defined the word of God as "God-breathed", and he went on to say that it is a most useful tool for teaching, rebuking, correcting and training children in righteousness. He says; any child who had been adequately schooled in the word of God would become thoroughly equipped for every good work to the glory of God:

Because, according to Solomon, a child who pays attention to his parents' instructions and teachings will not only gain understanding; but, will invariably maintain discretion in all his dealings in life; even as his lips will preserve knowledge always, Proverbs 5:2.

Observe that it is of utmost benefits therefore to teach our children the fear of God; because like He had said to David in the ancient past, He says to every child today; "I will guide thee with mine eye." In other words, God is simply telling us that He knows the exact number of hairs on every child's head, Matt 10:30; He knows when the child sorrows, Exodus 3:7:

That He indeed records every child's tears, Psalm 56:8; takes notes of every child's down sitting and uprisings (Psalm 139:2). Even that, all a child's thoughts, ways and words are known to Him, Psalm 139 2-6. And, according to Malachi 3:16, know that your child's name will, no doubt, be in the book of remembrance being written before Him of those who fear Him and think upon His name. So take it upon yourself as a parent to school your child on the fear of God-righteous living – it's only the fear of God that opens the door for God's guidance.

Let me leave you here with a beautiful prayer I found in the scriptures' book of Hebrews. I presume that this prayer, as you delight yourself in rendering it unto God always, will help a great deal in causing your child to grow up to have the fear of God Almighty:

May the God of peace, who through the blood of the eternal covenant brought back from the dead our Lord Jesus, that great Shepherd of the sheep equip you (mention your child's name) with everything good for doing his will.

And may he work in (you) us what is pleasing to him, through Jesus Christ, to whom be glory forever and ever, Amen. Hebrews 13:20-21.

Make Your Child Become An Adult - Member of Church At Twelve

The age of twelve, which is usually assumed to be the beginning of the adolescent period for growing children, is what I always like to refer to as; "the age of identity". This is the age, save for female children who maybe a year or two faster than their male counterparts, at which a young person's sexual organs and reproductive systems begin to develop so as to become capable of having children. This age of transformation is often referred to as the age of puberty.

A child before puberty is only but a child, and must be handled and cared for by the parents as such. But, the signs of transformation that occur at puberty, usually, would generate such thoughts like; "oh! I too will soon be like mum or dad", that is, become an adult, in a child. And so, it must be realized that the adolescent stage of the child's life, which closely follows puberty, always presents a delicate bridge that parents must endeavor to help their children cross cautiously if they must arrive safely on the other side of their lives – the adult stage.

Observe that apart from the physical changes in the child's body chemistry that will normally begin to occur here, the young person's peculiar demeanor will also begin to find some avenue for expression. Surely, you will remember how the Lord Jesus Christ as a twelve-year- old boy, had shocked His parent with His passion for God's word and work in a little story told in Luke Chapter two.

This story has it that Jesus, as a boy of twelve had stayed back in Jerusalem after a particular Passover feast, unknown to His parents. Now, I have two vital issues to draw from this story. Firstly, realize that it is because there is usually that tendency for every twelve-year- old child to exhibit similar behavior, that is, to try to make a statement behaviorally that, yes, I have arrived at the adult scene, I am capable of doing things myself now; is the reason I often tell people that the age of twelve is the "age of identity".

The other issue flowing from the boy Jesus' defection mentioned above is that, I got a revelation that this particular Passover Ceremony was the first Jesus was to attend as a participator and a mature member of God's holy assembly. Nehemiah revealed that such important Israelites' congregations usually comprised men, women and all who could hear with understanding, Nehemiah 8:2. At the age of twelve, for instance, the Muslims make it mandatory for their children to participate actively in the yearly Ramadan fast.

Perhaps, Jesus might have attended several Passover Feasts before attaining the age of twelve, but no mention is made of any other in the Gospels save for the particular one he had attended with His parents as recorded in Luke 2:42. Jesus was a super twelve-year-old boy, one who had come to teach the world God's ways.

And being God's son, I believe He had intelligently calculated and designed that occasion of His first formal participation in the Passover Ceremony to give an early specimen of what God had given Him commission to do on earth to His parents, and indeed, to the general public. This brings me to the biblical truth I want to share with you here in this chapter; the Passover feast, its importance as it concerns our twelve-year-old children.

You will find in Exodus 12:1 – 27 the record of how God had instituted the feast of Passover for the Israelites to observe. It was a religious ceremony which was meant at the outset to acknowledge God's goodness to them, not only in preserving them from, but in delivering them by, the plaques He had inflicted on the Egyptians prior to their Exodus from Egypt. This feast had been established through Moses, and God had said it was to be a lasting ordinance – to be observed by all Israelites from generation to generation – see verse 14.

Now, what is in this particular Passover Ceremony Jesus had attended at age twelve, you might want to know. What in actual fact makes it a novelty? I believe Luke had had to feature it prominently in his records because of the very vital lesson it presents for us to learn, so that we can also observe it in this era of contemporary Christianity.

Moreover, I read in Matthew Henry's commentary how Jewish doctors and theologians have revealed that in the past, at twelve years old, it used to be mandatory for the children of the Israelites to begin to fast from time to time; and that at thirteen years old, a child was always expected to begin to be a son of the commandments: that is, to be obliged to the duties of adult church-membership, having been from his infancy, by virtue of his circumcision and consecration, a son of the covenant.

Christians, and especially parents, should realize that inducting a child into adult church-membership through the Passover Ceremony is a milestone, besides circumcision and consecration; our children must be made to observe in order to grow into godly, obedient and responsible adults. I implore you to peruse the following scripture verses, so as to catch the revelation that, indeed, a growing child should have his inaugural participation in the Passover Ceremony at the age of twelve:

> *Every year His (Jesus') parents went to*
> *Jerusalem for the feast of the Passover.*
>
> *When He (Jesus) was twelve years old, they*
> *(He and His parents) went up to the feast,*
> *according to the custom.- Luke 2:41 – 42.*

Notice that in verse 41 above, this scripture didn't record or say that Jesus was ever with His parents in previous years when they usually attended the yearly Passover feast. This is not to say that He (Jesus) as a boy of less than twelve wasn't always with them. I believe Luke didn't mention His presence at these previous yearly meetings because He was never reckoned as a participator as He was then under-aged. But, it behooved Luke to record for posterity, the Lord's (as a boy of twelve) first formal attendance of the feast of the Passover, as a qualified participator.

To gain a better insight as to the point I am making here, I implore you to place some emphasis on the words "He" and "they" in the quotation above. Or, better still, endeavor to replace them with the juxtaposed words in brackets for a clearer understanding.

Here is a sample of what is required to induct our twelve-year-old children into adult church membership. I have offered this here for preachers' use:

A Prayer Format For Inducting Your Children To Adult Church Membership At Age Twelve (A.K.A Gospel Passover Ceremony).

Both parents of the twelve-year-old present child before the preacher, and the child is made to answer the following questions unassisted by the preacher:

A. Preacher: *(Mention inductee's Name here) Do you believe that Jesus is the only begotten son of God?*

Inductee's Response: *Yes, I do believe.*

B. Preacher Do you believe that Jesus shed His blood,

and lay down His life, on the cross to save you from the bondage of sin and death?

Inductee's Response: Yes, I do believe.

C. Preacher

Do you want to have Jesus Christ of Nazareth as your Lord and Master throughout your lifetime?

Inductee's Response: Yes.

D. The preacher concludes thus:

O Lord God most High, Maker of the entire universe, I present to you today (MASTER/ MISS...) Son or daughter of MR/MRS.... in this Gospel Passover Ceremony in accordance with your word in Exodus 12:24.

I ask that you feed this child with the flesh, even as you fill him with the blood, of your Son Jesus.

For His flesh is real food and His blood real drink (John 6:54-55). Do this, O God, so this child maybe spiritually strengthened and nourished to

> *live a holy life acceptable to you. I Pray In The*
> *Name Of Jesus Christ Of Nazareth, Amen.*

Note that this freewill confession as in this question and answer session here is very vital to the Gospel Passover induction. The twelve-year-old, having been a member of the church since infancy, is expected to confess his understanding of, and belief in, God's salvation work for humanity.

In Exodus 12:27b, I read that the Israelites had bowed down and worshiped God after Moses and Aaron had relayed all the instructions instituting the Passover Feast to them. And in Luke 22:28, Jesus referred to His disciples as, "those who have stood by me in my trials." This apparently means that these disciples had accepted God's word through Him, and had believed absolutely in it. Hence they had merited to sit at the table with the Lord Jesus to observe the special last (Lord's) super.

To have denoted this particular family meal the Lord had had with His disciples as the; "Last Super" or "Lord's Super" was simply to differentiate the new order from the old. The Lord came into the world to consummate the transition God begun with Moses from the old order to the new order. Because Jesus had come as the reality of the law God gave through Moses, as He alone had said, He had come to fulfill them, Matthew 5:17.

And so, today's Christianity does not require us to slaughter animals in holy sacrifice to God as the Old Testament saints were made to do. The Lord Jesus' sacrifice of Himself on the Cross at Calvary was for the forgiveness of our sins, John 1:29; and for the satisfaction of our Passover needs, see 1 Cor. 5:7.

Understand then that what the Lord had done when He offered the cup as the new covenant in His blood, and the broken bread as His body, at the Lord's Super was a switch from the old to the new order, from the age-long Passover feast to the Gospel Passover.

And, when you recollect that Gospel, in a nutshell, actually means the teachings of Jesus and of the Apostles, then, you would understand that in contemporary Christianity, consecration of anything, even our bodies and souls, is to be done now by the word of God through prayer (in the name of Jesus) – see 1 Timothy 4:5. So, to consecrate ourselves (children or adults) to God through observance of the Gospel Passover, therefore, is not to slaughter lambs, or to share man-made bread in our churches, but by praying.

Spiritual Benefits Of Inducting Twelve-Year-Old Children Into Adult Church-Membership

The importance of having to induct every twelve year-old child into adult church-membership can simply not be overemphasized. Because at this age of twelve, which I have already described as the "age of identity" at the beginning of this chapter, God gets to beam heaven's searchlights on the child to transform him/her both bodily and psychologically, or spiritually if you like.

The Gospel Passover, therefore, when conducted, will make for the child's spiritual transformation into being an adult member of God's holy family. Below are further benefits there are in this Christian Ceremony for our twelve-year-old children:

(1) The ancient Passover feast had been commanded by God to act as a mark of separation of the Israelites from the Egyptians; and to provide them with security in times of trouble. See Exodus 12:27.

(2) Any child inducted into adult church-membership today, would be sure of divine security in times of trouble, he/she would have his/her conscience pacified; plus be marked for God and, thus, be given that boldness of access to God's throne of grace.

(3) A spiritual wall of protection would be formed round any child who observes the Gospel Passover; and thus, a wall of partition between him and the children of this world who would otherwise have had bad influence on him.

(4) Because the Gospel Passover does pacify conscience, a twelve-year old child who observes it would become protected from the wrath of God, the curse of the law, and the damnation of hell, Romans 8:1.

(5) A child inducted into adult church-membership will not be given to disobedience and rebellion, like the children of this world, because he will always remain in Jesus and Jesus in him, John 6:56.

(6) And because it's a protection from the wrath of God, the curse of the law, and the damnation of hell; any child who observes the gospel Passover has the Lord's promise of eternal life – See this promise of the Lord in the scriptures thus:

Whoever eats my flesh and drinks my blood has eternal life, and I will raise him up at the last day – John 6:54

Now, let me conclude here without any iota of equivocation that children, if in their infancy were dedicated to God, should be called upon, as a matter of divine necessity, when they are grown-up to come to the (Lord's Super) Gospel Passover: This is so that they might make it their own act and deed to join themselves to the Lord forever.

Observe that a farmer who doesn't leave the very fragile tendrils of his growing yams in his farm to creep on the ground, but stakes them, does so because he desires to have a good harvest. Such a farmer knows that to wish his growing crops well by staking them is equal to his hope for a profitable reward for his labor.

The Gospel Passover induction ceremony for your child is like staking the young tendrils of your growing yams in your farm. A word, they often say, is enough for the wise.

Chapter Eight

God Always Locates A Godly Child

When you begin with Abel and until Jesus, the Bible is replete with the names of people God had used as His godly seeds to carry out His work on earth – I mean personalities the Bible does bear their records as having been able to please God greatly because they had led holy and righteous lives.

And of all these godly personalities, a clear distinction can always be made between those God had located and used because they had been reared as godly children, and those He had sent to their parents to be specially raised for His use in carrying out some special projects on earth. In the former group, we have the likes of Noah, Abraham, Moses, Daniel, David, etc; and in the latter group, we have personalities like Samson – See Judges 13:5, John the Baptist See Luke 1:11-17, and the Lord Jesus Christ – See Luke 1:28-33.

I have made this distinction here in order to let you know that, whether human beings do have the spiritual insight and initiative to collaborate with God in raising godly children in the world or not, He's always able to locate His special seeds on earth. And that, He is ever so delighted to find a godly seed for His use anytime He does have a special task to be done, because when He can not find any who had been raised in righteousness like Noah, He will simply provide Himself with one, like His begotten son, Jesus.

As parents, we should realize that, indeed, the onus is on us to fulfill our side of the bargain, as co-workers with God, in the business of rearing our children. We must realize that having a good understanding of God and His word is paramount to being able to instruct, teach, control and guide our children in the way to live righteously – to have the fear of God: for God only locates and identifies with someone who lives righteously.

Dare To Make Your Child A Godly Seed

Friend, do you know that God, in His infinite wisdom and love, does always have a plan designed for every child born into the world? Man is God's master piece, His most prized investment on earth, and so that His definite plan maybe fulfilled in the life of everyone born into the world, God desires that every child be raised as a godly child. See what He had told Jeremiah as recorded in the Scriptures thus:

For I know the plans I have for you, declares the Lord, plans to prosper you and not to harm you, plans to give you hope and a future. Jeremiah 29:11.

God definitely foresees and anticipates every person's coming into the world. Instances abound in the scriptures which clearly reveal that God always does have a plan prepared for each child before it is conceived and born into the world. This was true of John the Baptist; and, indeed, many others we have read of in the Bible. Jeremiah 1:4-5, for instance, tells us of how God had spoken about His foreknowledge of Jeremiah and his future while he was still in his mother's womb.

Now, if this is true as the scriptures reveal, then, of course, it is a truth of immense importance. And this truth, I must say, should be the ruling passion of all parents, whether Christians or non-Christians, to endeavor to bring up their children the godly way; because every child bred the godly way will invariably grow up to fulfill his destiny ultimately.

You ought to be delighted to know that what raising your children the godly way does entail is to hand them over to the Lord Jesus, because He is the one who gives understanding. John had revealed that the son of God has already come and has given the world understanding, so that everyone who believes may know Him who is true. Hence, every believer is in Him who is true – even in His son Jesus Christ- who is the true God, and eternal life – 1 John 5:20.

And observe also that when the Lord Jesus had said, "I am the way and the truth and the life", He meant that in Him, and through Him, we find the definite way to please God Almighty in everything we do; that He is the way to righteous living and, to a fulfilled life. No human being can ever amount to anything apart from Jesus, John 15:5.

I have said; "in Him", as above, because all the spiritual exercises that Jesus underwent when He came as one of us present practical examples of what we ought to do to prosper and profit profoundly in our godly walk and work on earth. And I have also said; "through him", because the Lord Jesus it was who had come with the truth from God to enlighten the world on how to hook up with heaven in order to succeed the godly way in everything we do, including the upbringing of our children. See what Isaiah had said of the Savior thus"

I am the Lord your God, who teaches you what is best
for you, who directs you in the way you should go.
- Isaiah 48:17.

You Should Ask God For His Leading And Direction To Raise Your Child As A Godly Seed

Before I proceed to state, in a nutshell, those religious rites you must have your growing child observe in order that he/she might grow up to become a godly child, let me quickly note here that the fundamental reason many people have failed, and keep failing, in rearing their children as godly children, is because they never ask God for His leading or direction.

Meanwhile, in John 16:23, the Lord Jesus had taught that God grants whatever request we ever make of Him, as long as it conforms with His word. And James, following his understanding of this scripture, had taught that if anyone lacks wisdom, even the wisdom to bring up our children the godly way, he/she should ask God. He says God never fails to give generously, and without finding fault, to everyone who asks Him – See James 1:5.

So, the problem with us today, why a lot of people cannot raise their offspring as obedient and godly children in our world, is because they never ask God to grant them the wisdom to do so; because they do not ask for God's direction and leading, and because they do not realize that, indeed, they ought to practically ask God to be the chief executive officer in the undertaking.

Here, let me show you two couples, from the scriptures, who had had the necessary insight and initiative to ask for God's leading and direction in the business of raising their children the godly way. The first couple is Mr. and Mrs. Manoah, Samson's parents; and the other couple is Mr. and Mrs. Elkanah, Samuel's parents. Both couples had displayed a high sense of imitable initiative and understanding of God and His ways.

In the scriptures' book of Judges chapter thirteen and verse three (Judges 13:3), you will find the story of how an angel of God had appeared to Mrs. Manoah to announce to her that, even though she was sterile and had thus remained childless for a long while, she was going to conceive and have a son. And how later, when Mrs. Manoah relayed her encounter with an angel of the Lord to her husband, perhaps, out of anxiety, he had prayed thus:

Then Manoah prayed to the Lord: "O Lord, I beg you, let the man of God you sent to us come again to teach us how to bring up the boy who is to be born - Judges 13:8.

And afterwards, when God answered his prayer and allowed His angel to return to them, Mr. Manoah had promptly cashed in on the situation to ask for God's leading and direction from the messenger of God. See what he had promptly prayed God for thus:

> *So Manoah asked him (the angel), "when your*
> *words are fulfilled what is to be the rule for*
> *the boy's life and work?" - Judges 13:12.*

You will observe in the handling of this matter by the Manoahs a rare expression of optimism towards being able to raise their coming little boy as a godly seed for God. Note also that because they had realized, at the very outset, that the obstacle was probably going to be their ignorance in this regard, they earnestly asked for God's spiritual enlightenment, so as to insure success in the task of raising their son.

Now, the other couple I have mentioned above is Mr. and Mrs. Elkanah, Samuel's parents in the scriptures – See story in 1 Samuel 1. The Bible account under reference here says Hannah had prayerfully gotten a little boy from God and she had named the boy Samuel. Afterwards, she and her husband, Elkanah, had given up their son to live with an aged priest named Eli, so that he could worship the Lord in His house all the days of his life – V 28.

No doubt, these couples, Samson's parents, as well as Samuel's present themselves as role models that contemporary parents should strive to emulate concerning the very critical task of bringing up children the godly way today. You will notice that the Manoahs, knowing that they were ignorant of matters of God, were not ashamed to ask for God's collaboration.

The Elkanahs, on the other hand, because they didn't want to fail in the proper and godly upbringing of their son, had had their little boy, Samuel, planted promptly in God's House after he was weaned. Observe that this couple, who can not however be said to have been wanting in their understanding of matters of God, had decided to give up their little boy because, they hadn't wanted to bring him up by trial and error. The Elkanahs had been portrayed as a godly family in this story under reference, that Hannah as in 1 Samuel 1:11, had had the understanding and intelligence to make a vow to God, promising to give up her son to Him after he would have been born also adequately supports this view.

Let me liken the action of the Manoahs in the story about the birth of Samson above to a scenario in which a scholar decides to beg his professor overseeing his project for useful hints before commencing a scholarly work; and that of the Elkanahs, also, to the action of a little child in a kindergarten class who comes home from school with homework he feels he can not handle and decides to beg an elder sibling, or his parent to assist him: Either action here is bottom-lined by the desire for glowing success; a burning desire to excel.

Becoming A Success As A Godly Adult

The child who has been raised the godly way will now, at maturity, observe the final Christian rites of saying the prayer for salvation, getting baptized in water, and the Holy Spirit, in order that he/she becomes a consummated Christian or believer. And becoming a consummated believer means that the individual is now available for God's blessing and perpetual guidance. Here is one very important thing Christians need to know when they mature in their godly walk: God's blessings for the believer will only begin to manifest with accepting or confessing Jesus formally as Lord and Savior.

Now, we know that the Bible is rather silent on the two critical issues regarding the extent to which children should participate in church activities before they're considered mature in Christianity, and the time and age a person is expected to get born again; but, however, I do have some reliable opinion to share with you here.

As for the first issue of the extent to which children should participate in church activities before becoming adult Christians, I could bet that there is no other foundation more suitable for the young Christian than the foundation of faith in Jesus Christ I have suggested on the pages of this book so far.

Regarding being born again, on the other hand, I would suggest very strongly that it should be done when a believer has attained the age of thirty. Jesus, Himself had had his baptism in water and the Holy Spirit when He was about the age of thirty, Luke 3:23. And so old the Scriptures say Joseph was when he had entered the services of Pharaoh, King of Egypt – Genesis 41:46.

And I read in 2 Samuel 5:4, that David was thirty(30) years old when he began to reign over Israel as king. And in fact, Numbers 4:3 records that this was the age God had stipulated for the ancient Jewish priests to enter upon the full execution of their priestly duties.

Having highlighted these very crucial truths as above, let me quickly tell you here that the only thing I have simply tried to do, so far in this book, is point the right way to lay a firm foundation in Christianity for our children so they can grow up to become responsible, obedient and godly adults in the service of God in our societies.

Know that confessing Jesus Christ as Lord and Savior plus the baptism of water and the Holy Spirit is the final Christian Ceremony every adult member of the church must undergo. To confess Jesus as Lord and Savior renders the believer's sins covered by the precious blood of the Savior, and thus, makes the individual qualified to stand before God justified, because he/she has been covered with Jesus' robe of righteousness.

Note that it is only a Christian who wears this robe of righteousness that is entitled to rendering his years in pleasure and prosperity; because, as prophet Isaiah had revealed, God only blesses believers who are willing and obedient, and His best from the land is reserved for them alone – See Isaiah 2:17. Know that Jesus' robe of righteousness meets God's conditions for holiness; and to meet God's conditions for holiness means that you are available and qualified for heaven's blessings.

Having been raised as a child of God, the mature believer should realize that Jesus has fulfilled the law at cavalry so that all who believe could enjoy the blessings that come through righteousness. Jesus bore the penalty of all believers' sins in His own body on the cross; therefore, every believer is redeemed from sin's curse on humanity because of Jesus' shed blood on the cross, See 1 Peter 1:18-19 and Revelations 5:9.

Benefits Of Walking With Jesus As A Godly Adult

Tremendous benefits abound for everyone who has consciously undergone the various stages of development I have revealed in this book, and has attained maturity in Christianity. Amongst these benefits are:

Firstly, the believer will be enabled to serve God without fear in holiness and righteousness before Him all the days of his life – Luke 1:74b, 75; because the Lord shall guide his feet perpetually into the path of peace – v. 79b. God says, He will make his path straight – Proverb 3:6, because he has accepted Jesus as his Lord and Savior, and having been raised as a godly child, Jesus resides in him and gives him an abundant life: which means, having more than enough, more than he/she would ever need because a life spent with the Lord means a life of great abundance, but, one without Him means, poverty and total deprivation, John 10:10.

A third blessing you will enjoy having been religiously reared from childhood to adulthood as a godly seed (child) is that, there will be healing in every area of your life:

He himself bore our sins in his body on the tree, so that we might die to sins and live for righteousness; by his wounds you have been healed- 1 Peter 2:24.

Also, having been raised through Jesus Christ, you have abundant prosperity. You will prosper physically, spiritually, and temporarily when you recognize and receive Jesus as God's seed of righteousness given to the world in whom all blessings are embodied:

*But seek ye first the Kingdom of God, and his righteousness,
and all these things shall be added unto you.
(Matthew 6:33) KJV.*

*But my God shall supply all your need according to his
riches in glory by Christ Jesus – Philippians 4:19.*

Chapter Nine

Christians Fail For Lack Of Knowledge

"Jesus didn't complete His assignment on earth; as He was killed by the devil, this is the reason He is scheduled to come back to the world."

These are the absolutely incredible words a man old enough to be my father had said to me the other day during a discussion session. To say that I was greatly amazed to hear these words from the mouth of someone who has been a professed Christian for decades is simply an understatement.

And you know what! After I had listened to this man speak, the obvious reality of the prophet Hosea's stark revelation in Hosea 4:6 as to the reason people of God fail, and are usually destroyed by the evil one in the world, dawned on me. Hosea, while speaking God's mind, had revealed that:

> *(God's people)My people are destroyed from*
> *lack of knowledge. – Hosea 4:6.*

In other words, the reason people often stray from the paths of God, cannot live fulfilled lives, why they suffer pain, poverty, retrogression, etc. and can not generally enjoy the life of abundance Jesus came to provide for the entire humanity through His salvation work, is because they lack knowledge of the enormous love and care God holds for every human being on earth.

Now, people do not seem to understand that ignorance of God and his ways breeds disobedience, and that disobedience invariably leads to a departure from God's standards. I read in Isaiah 53:6 that if human beings had not turned from God's ways, and had not started desiring the satisfaction of their own ways, Jesus would not have come to sacrifice Himself on the cross.

The good thing with this sacrifice however is that, heaven has released our inheritance bequeathed to us by our Savior. But do Christians realize this? Because, still, people continue to live unhappy and defeated lives on earth because they prefer their own ways to God's ways wherein lie abundant life – John 10:10. The untenable excuse people often give for preferring to chart their own way, like Esau in the scriptures, is that, it is too cumbersome to live righteously to please God. How sad!

No doubt, you would remember Esau in the scriptures. It was because he was ignorant of the things of God that he had lost his inheritance to his younger sibling, Jacob, as the first son of Isaac. You will agree with me that his overriding preference, and passion, had been for less importance matters; like having a thriving career in hunting, and for food.

Esau had foolishly ignored the enormous benefit he was to derive from taking over his father's estate as the first son; and so, without exercising any restraint he had willing turned his birthright, his inheritance right as the first son, over to his brother in exchange for a paltry pot of porridge- read story in Genesis chapter twenty seven.

And, as you would have read in Hebrews12:17, afterwards, when he wanted to inherit this blessing he was rejected. Observe also that, the author of Hebrews, on account of Esau's disgraceful behavior, had equally described him as a godless person, verse16. In other words, to be ignorant of God and His ways is synonymous to being godless.

Parents, especially professed Christians, should note, therefore, that it amounts to godlessness if they do not have good knowledge and understanding of our ever helpful God for profitable Christian walk and work; and that it is godlessness if they do not, or can not, rear their children as godly, obedient, and responsible people capable of making the much desired positive change in the world situation today.

People should realize that when they do not teach their children, when they are young, to remember their creator, they cannot expect that their creator should remember their children when they grow old. God gives children to honor marriages, but if couples dishonor Him with that which is their honor, then, sooner or later, they are turned into shame, or become laughing stock to them—for God says those that despise Him shall be lightly esteemed, see 1 Samuel 2:30 KJV.

We live in a world, and in an age, today in which the good Lord, Jesus, is completely rejected. And, ironically, there is nothing around us that can give us real peace, joy, and satisfaction besides the Lord: the Scriptures say every man is doomed to failure outside of Jesus, John 15:5. I tell you that, indeed, Jesus alone is the God-given solution to the human problem.

Know that Jesus, who is the living word of God, is the only one who can and will make your child a victor. He alone is capable of making diseases, sicknesses, and poverty your child's servants when you connect him to the Lord. Because, connecting the child to Jesus means bringing God on the scene in his life, it means that the child would be highly privileged to have the living word in his lips. And it is the living word in your child's lips that will bring victory, joy, and success; instead of defeat in his life.

Believers need to understand clearly what the Lord had meant when He said; "IT IS FINISHED" (John 19:30), while on the cross at Cavalry. It meant that His work as a dying sacrifice for us had been completed. Understand, therefore, that what had been insinuated by this announcement was that following His victory over Satan and his kingdom, He would be requiring living sacrifices to carry on His work on earth. And you know what, you and I, all believers, are those living sacrifices.

If our children must become living sacrifices for God's work therefore; then, they must be dedicated to God at birth. This act of presentation and dedication of our children I preach here right now is what is expected to lead to a process of continuous devotedness to God until the child gets baptized ultimately at adulthood.

And it will interest you to know that every child dedicated to the Lord, and taught the very vital lessons about the fear of God, that is, how to live righteously, while growing up, will learn to trust in God always to be entire, exclusive, transfiguring and, eventually, become fulfilled in the Lord.

In the book of proverbs, it is revealed that to have understanding (of God's word and ways) is tantamount to having a fountain of life; whereas, punishment (that is, a life of bitterness, lack and unhappiness) is the portion of anyone who lacks it, Proverbs 16:22.

In an epistle to Timothy, his dear son in the ministry, Paul had written a very sound, and quite fatherly, counsel urging him to practice only what he had learnt from infancy until maturity from the Holy scriptures. And elsewhere, in a separate letter to the Romans, he had also advised believers to always endeavor to preserve and present themselves as living sacrifices for God's use. See both scriptures thus:

> *In fact, everyone who wants to live a godly life*
> *in Christ Jesus will be persecuted,.…*
> *But as for you, continue in what you have*
> *learned and have become convinced of,.…*
> *And how from infancy you have known the Holy Scriptures,*
> *which are able to make you wise for salvation through*
> *faith in Christ Jesus - 2 Timothy 3:12, 14a, 15.*
> *Therefore, I urge you, brothers, in view of God's mercy,*
> *to offer your bodies as living sacrifices, holy and pleasing*
> *to God – this is your spiritual act of workshop.-*
> *Romans 12:1*

Now, I have already talked about those fundamental rites and/or ceremonies believers must observe from infancy until maturity previously in this book. Understand that these rites, which I did say should climax with the baptism in water and the Holy Spirit, are the acts by which every human being born into the world must turn his/her body over to God, once and for all, to be His for whatever purpose He may have for him/her.

The acts by which, according to Paul in Romans 12:1 above, we offer our bodies as living sacrifices, holy and pleasing to our God.

You Must Discern God's Word Correctly For Maximum Benefits

The "word of God" is a term often used to refer to the will of God for humanity revealed to us. Literally, it describes the Bible, and it is synonymous with "The Holy Scriptures." But, when put simply, the word of God is God's disclosure of Himself and His truth to mankind.

Now, not many Christians realize that to fully gain understanding of the word of God and have it work profitably in their lives; they must approach it from two perspectives: there is the word of God in principles as in the law God had given through Moses, and the word of God as a reality revealed in the person of Jesus Christ. See what Jesus had said while making this clarification thus:

> *Do not think that I have come to abolish the law or the prophets; I have not come to abolish them but to fulfill them.- Matthew 5:17.*

If you believed Moses, you would believe me,
for he wrote about me – John 5:46.

This clarification made in these scriptures above notwithstanding, what we do find in our churches today is unnecessary religiosity – people holding on to the old testament law, and man-made dogmas, rather than to Jesus who is the reality of the law. Now, let me ask you here, between a photocopy and an original which should be preferable? Which should every rational-mined person be delighted to have?

No doubt, every sane human being would choose to have an original rather than a photocopy. Your photograph, for instance, is at best just a copy of yourself. And this means, in other-words, that a copy is usually nothing more than a representation of the subject's reality. Now, while making the clarification between Moses' law and Jesus as the reality, the author of the Bible's book of Hebrews had said;

The law is only a shadow of the good things that are
coming – not the realities themselves. – Hebrews 10:1a.

And a renowned twentieth century preacher, E.W Kenyon, had also referred to the law through Moses, which is being relied upon by human beings in almost every endeavor of life today, as the, "the sense knowledge." And he had called the knowledge that comes from God through Jesus the reality of the law, the Revelation knowledge."

Kenyon had suitably reported the negative impact of man's inability to connect with Jesus, who is the reality of the law, in our human endeavors; and he said the church, especially, has been greatly0020affected. Hear his own words thus:

> *The unhappy fact is that "Sense knowledge" had gained the supremacy in the church. The church is a spiritual organization, a spiritual body, to be governed through the spirit instead of the senses.*
>
> *When sense knowledge gained ascendancy in the church and the fountain of the church, the theological school, the church ceased to be a spiritual body and simply became a body of men governed by sense knowledge.*
>
> *The chief quest of sense knowledge has been for reality. Man's spirit craves it. Reality cannot be found by senses. It is only discovered by the spirit.*

And in John 6:63, the master Himself had taught that; *The spirit (Jesus and the Holy Spirit God gives through Him) gives lives; the flesh (the law) counts for nothing. The words I have spoken to you are spirit and they are life.*

Observe that I have carefully juxtaposed the words in brackets as in the above scripture to make for better insight. Jesus says even though you have had the entire Bible committed to your memory, you only have but the word in principles, which counts for nothing. He says to be up to something meaningful in your life, you must have the spirit (the reality of God's word for mankind, Jesus Himself) in the inside of you. In other words, the spirit in the scriptures' verse above is synonymous with Jesus, just as the flesh is used to refer to the law of Moses. No wonder, the Lord had said; "apart from me you can do nothing – John 15:5".

Behold! Jesus Is At The Threshold Of Every Man's Heart Knocking.

It is always a delight to me each time I remember that many of the multitude of promises God had handed down through His ancient prophets to His followers on earth have already been faithfully fulfilled. Every Bible scholar knows that, beginning from Genesis to Revelations, God's divine promises to us abound; but, unfortunately, not many understand that many of them, like I said, have been met already. Here, let me show you one of such great promises of God as had been revealed by the prophet Jeremiah and which has already been fulfilled:

"This is the covenant I will make with the house of Israel after that time, declares the Lord.

I will put my laws in their minds and write them on their hearts. I will be their God, and they will be my people.

No longer will a man teach his neighbor, or a man his brother, saying, 'know the Lord,' because they will all know me, from the least of them to the greatest.

For I will forgive their wickedness and will remember their sins no more."- Jeremiah 31:33 – 34.

Now, it is often not clearly realized by many that what God had here in this scripture above promised He had also faithfully fulfilled already through Jesus, His son, in the Gospel time. And because people lack this understanding, I found out that, it is doubtlessly right to conclude also that they do not understand that the particular articles of this new covenant God had promised His people all contain spiritual blessings.

There is a general consensus amongst biblical writers that Jesus had indeed come to satisfy this new covenant needs for God's people; that He has come to fulfill and complete the reconciliation with God begun at Mount Sinai. In 1 Corinthians 11:25, Paul wrote that Jesus had called the cup He had offered to His disciples as; "this cup is the new covenant in my blood."

Also know that this new covenant through Christ Jesus is rightly observed in Hebrews 8:6 as one that is far superior to the old one because it was founded on better promises; and therefore, does have a spiritual undertone. You must observe that God hadn't said; "I will give them the land of Canaan and a numerous issue" as He had promised Abraham in Genesis 13:14-17, 15:12-21; to Isaac Genesis 26:1-6; and also to Jacob Genesis 28: 10 -22.

But He had said; "I will give them pardon, and peace, and grace, good heads, and good health", as He had once said to Moses while establishing the old covenant which has now become obsolete – Hebrews 8:13.

While echoing Jeremiah's message, the Bible's book of Hebrews explains that Christians no longer have to live by Old Testament regulations. The author also notes that, yes, the written law had been useful because it was God-given;

but that, as the history of Israel had proved, the law had lacked the power to transform people's inner attitudes.

The author explained that this was the reason God had been forced to decide that something more was needed, something that would change His people's thinking, nay, change them from inside out. Thus, God had settled on a new covenant, one that was to be far better than the old one; whereby He would put the law into the hearts of His people through His Holy Spirit, read Hebrews chapter eight. I tell you that this new covenant has already come in Christ Jesus – See Paul's revelation thus:

Now the Lord is the spirit, and where the
spirit of the Lord is, there is freedom.

And we, who with unveiled faces all reflect the Lord's
glory, are being transformed into his likeness with
ever- increasing glory, which comes from the Lord,
who is the spirit. – 2 Corinthians 3:17 – 18.

How much more, then, will the blood of Christ, who
through the eternal spirit offered Himself unblemished
to God, cleanse our consciences from acts that lead
to death, so that we may serve the living God.

For this reason Christ is the mediator of a new
covenant, that those who are called may receive the
promised eternal inheritance – now that He had died
as a ransom to set them free from the sins committed
under the first covenant. – Hebrews 9:14-15.

Jesus, in the light of this very intriguing reality, that is, that He Himself, was God's truth and will, as it is in heaven, who had come to the world so that all God's people on earth might have heaven's glory manifested in their lives, John 10:10, 14:6, had thrown an open invitation to all humanity, asking everyone to come to Him for the gift of His redemptive spirit thus:

> *"Come to me, all you who are weary and*
> *burdened, and I will give you rest.*
>
> *Take my yoke upon you and learn from me for I am gentle*
> *and humble in heart, and you will find rest for your souls.*
>
> *For my yoke is easy and my burden is*
> *light" - Matthew 11:28-30.*

This clarion call the Lord made here inviting all humanity to approach Him for His soothing peace is what A. W. Tozer had referred to as; "the doctrine of prevenient drawing". Prevenient drawing (or calling, if you like), briefly stated according to TOZER, means that before any man can seek God, God must first have sought {called or drawn} the man. And obviously God is here calling upon souls for redemption. The Lord is asking every man's soul, irrespective of race, color, and even religious affiliation, to come forth to be supernaturally fortified so as to become capable of living righteously.

And by this call or invitation of the Lord in the quotation above, He is simply telling us that He's at the door of everyone's heart knocking as revealed by John in

Revelations,3 :3a; He is asking you to open your heart so that He, who is God's living word, would come to indwell in you. Understand friend that, indeed, Jesus is God's Law that He had promised through the prophet Jeremaiah to imprint on people's minds and hearts, Jeremiah 31:33. The difference however is that Jesus is spiritual and the reality of the Law.

Quite interestingly, Paul, a new-testament preacher, had written in his epistles to the Colossians and the Romans about this truth. And recall also that Moses had earlier taught the same message to the Old Testaments Saints: Moses had revealed in Deuteronomy 30:6 that God will always, in all generations, circumcise the hearts of those who obey Him so they can love Him with all their heart and with all their soul, and live abundant lives.

I presume Paul was explaining this revelation made by Moses in Deuteronomy 30:6 to the Saints in Rome when he wrote that this circumcision is circumcision of the heart by the Spirit, and not by the written code. And elsewhere, in a letter to the Colossians he had further explained that in Jesus Christ we (believers) have been circumcised as in the putting off of the sinful nature; not with a circumcision done by the hands of men, but with the circumcision done by Christ – Colossians 2:11.

What a great pity that human beings are still so obstinately disposed to opening up their hearts for the Lord's indwelling! I suppose the problem is; a lot of people cannot imagine the magnitude of benefits they stand to gain from surrendering their entire lives to the Lord.

See what the Lord says are your benefits when you repent of your sins and accept Him as Lord of your life; He says; He and His Father, will love you immensely and will not hesitate for even a moment to come and make their home with you, John 14:23. And He says, even though you were doomed to death because of sin, having opened up your heart to God's living truth through repentance, you become qualified to have salvation come to dwell in your house – Luke 19:9.

Wow! What a great wonder, and indeed, a delight it would be for the Captain of God's salvation for humanity, Joshua 5:14, come to dwell in one's house. I just wish Zacchaeus were still around, his presence would definitely have presented Christians with the opportunity to take him to task on what it is like to host Jesus, the Captain of our Salvation, for a few hours; let alone, to have Him abide perpetually in one's house for ever. Isaiah 40:5 reveals that all mankind together will see God's salvation for us.

Chapter Ten

My Final Word For You

I mentioned in my preface of this book that my goal was to present on its pages the "how-to" make Jesus the foundation (beginning), the middle, and the end of the life of everyone born into the world. I want to believe that I have been able to achieve this objective. Well, let me leave you to be the judge in this.

But speaking frankly, it would be of utmost joy to me to know that, through writing this book, I have been able to contribute to the promotion of God's work on earth. I believe that anyone who reads this book would, no doubt, gain more insight as to how to groom children the proper way. Jesus is the reality of every promise God has ever made to mankind. Committing your child's life unto Jesus therefore is tantamount to making sure that he's set on the right pathway that invariably leads to enduring peace, plus abundant prosperity and success in this world.

Paul had taught in 2 Timothy 2:5 that if anyone competes as an athlete, he does not receive the victor's crown unless he competes according to the rules. Similarly, if you do desire that your child grows up to become a responsible, obedient and, indeed, a total success in life; then, you cannot afford to deny him/her the opportunity to observe the various Christian-rites I have revealed in this book.

To cast your child upon the Lord, for instance, which is one of the rites I have recommended, means to undertake to raise your child according to spiritual rules. It means to sow bountifully, to sow upon Jesus the Lord. And Paul says; "Now the Lord is the spirit, and where the spirit of the Lord is, there is freedom" – that is, freedom from the manipulation and influence of this evil world – 2 Corinthians 3:17.

Understand friend that, according to John Maxwell, "success isn't accumulating possessions, wealth, or power; but success is obeying God. It means having those close to you love and respect you the most."

Here is that perfect spiritual key, given in a nutshell, that you need to turn that precious little child given to you by God into a great success, and a total man or woman through Christ Jesus:

1. Endeavor to plant your newly born baby in your home in the name of the Lord Jesus Christ.
2. Ensure that your child is presented and consecrated to the Lord in God's house and in the presence of His holy assembly, the infant Jesus had been so presented and consecrated –see Luke 2: 22. Perhaps, you will be quick to disagree with me by arguing that the infant Jesus had been so presented and consecrated because He was the firstborn male child of Mary's womb, and as such His had been done

according to God's command in Exodus 13:2, 12; but, I like you to know that what had been made possible and, indeed available to all, when the Lord Jesus gave up His spirit on the cross was unrestricted access to God, see Hebrews 10:19—20.

3. Have your child observe his/her conversion from being a "child-member" of the Church to being an "adult-member" at the age of twelve {12}.

4. To be a totally successful man in Christ Jesus, your child who has become an adult-member of God's family should say the prayer for salvation or perform the all-important baptism in water, and experience the Holy Spirit baptism for his /her maximum benefit from his /her Christian walk.

Read This If You Have A Burning Desire To Please God With Your Life.

1. Always desire to do the right thing without any compromise.

2. Get rid of anything that isn't useful to your life and your godly walk. Learn not to ever waste your precious time and opportunities chasing after frivolities and trivialities.

You should realize that there are three very critical things in life that, once gone, never come back; and three others you should never lose. In the former group is time, words, and opportunity. And in the latter you have hope, peace, and honesty. These essentially, are the godly virtues that should drive our human societies to make for excellence.

3. Endeavor to imprint on your subconscious mind your belief or conviction that God can always heal everything, especially the so-called hopeless situations of our lives. Understand that however good or bad a situation might be, it will come to pass. It has definitely not come to stay- "no condition is permanent", people often say. Ensure that, no matter how you feel, you must always endeavor to get up, dress up and show up in order that defeat would have no place in your life. Consistency is the rule of life. The Lord Jesus Himself gave us the formula for success when He taught that we stay with it to the end- see Matthew 24:13 I tell you that God's best is yet to come. It is important that you develop a very good expectation of a favorable outcome in everything you do in life. Each time you awake in the morning, you should be moved to thank God, because life itself is his precious gift to us. In all things, and at all times, be joyful

God bless you!